Captain Buddha and his amazing Dukkha machine

A seven year journey

Ken Streat

This edition first published in January 2005
by Vasana Publishing,
PO Box 163,
Totnes, Devon, TQ9 7WY
UK

Book and cover design by Rick Lawrence
email: samskara@onetel.com

A catalogue record of this book is available from The British Library.

ISBN 0-9549489-0-4

Dukkha n. *(Pali/Sanskrit)* Suffering, the unsatisfactory
nature of things born of impermanence.
The first of the Four Noble Truths of Buddhism.

Acknowledgments

With thanks for all their support and encouragement to Siggi, Patrick, Rick, Dick and Dianna.

*It is in the nature of being to see adventure in becoming,
as it is in the very nature of becoming to seek peace in being.*

Sri Nisargadatta Maharaj

Chapter 1

IRAN 1976

They were right of course, I did love Miss Kate. The first time I saw her she was boarding the Iranian Air Force teachers' bus. She was small and slim in her flared corduroy jeans. She gave the driver a smile and moved down the aisle, pulling a face of amused surprise as the bus jolted into motion. She dropped into an empty seat and her cotton Benares scarf caught over the seat back, and hung there, fluttering like a veil in the hot air. There were two types of teacher on the bus; those with qualifications who had been flown out directly from England on two year contracts, and the travellers. The travellers had been passing through, coming or going between Asia and Europe. I had picked up a shirt and tie in the bazaar, handed over thirty six passport photographs to immigration, signed the six month contract and had become an Imperial Iranian Air Force English Instructor. Six months seemed a long time; it was hard for me to imagine that far into the future.

I was in the first days of my first class with twenty technical cadets. I was nineteen, and my own hated school days were still a fresh memory. Now, like my students, I could hardly believe I was an English teacher. As I struggled to keep the class in some semblance of order, the door opened from the adjoining classroom and in walked Kate, the girl from the bus. Could she borrow my black board cleaner? As the door closed behind her the class erupted.

'Instructor! Miss Kate is beautiful!'

'Mr Ken, do you love her?'

I felt myself beginning to blush. The class went mad with delight.

'You do! You do!'

'Mr Ken loves Miss Kate! Mr Ken loves Miss Kate!'

Kate was American and, like me, was travelling without itinerary or goal, just travelling for its own sake, a way of life that felt intoxicatingly free. During our breaks at work and on the bus we chatted, exchanging stories. She had been teaching for a couple of months, but had recently moved to my district from another Air Force base in the east of the city. I began visiting her in the evenings and weekends. We both worked the afternoon shift at the Air Force language school. We started work at two pm and finished at eight. We seldom went to bed before three or got up before mid-day. It was an ideal schedule.

With Kate the small things of life became remarkable. Her openness, beauty and light-the-world smile seemed to attract love and to draw out happiness. The simple activities of life, like going for walks or visits to the bazaar, were transformed, touched by her magic. We often walked the deserted city streets in the early hours, accompanied by packs of wild dogs that came in from the desert to scavenge at night. At first they were cautious, expecting stones or blows, but the friendliness we showed them made them wildly affectionate and instantly devoted. Each evening they would come running up, crowding around us, their tails wagging, wanting a bliss fix of pats and strokes. It felt to me as if they too were delighting in our love.

Kate took pleasure in who and what I was in a way I had never experienced before. She was twenty three, and she told me it was wonderful that I was already travelling at nineteen. She delighted in my English accent, she praised my drawings and paintings, she admired my clothes and told me they were beautiful. Through Kate's eyes I began to see new possibilities of who I was, or what I might become. The person Kate enjoyed was a surprise to me, I had no idea I possessed such desirable qualities. So I began dressing to please her, drawing and painting to impress her. I knew Kate didn't love me the way I loved her, but I didn't expect her to. She was so beautiful and so experienced, it was obvious she could not be expected to love me as I was. I was jealous, clingy and insecure. To be loved by Kate, to be needed by her, I knew I would have to change. I would have to be strong, detached and cool. I had set out from my ship and begun to swim to the siren; she sweetly beckoned me on, but I was already floundering in the strong currents.

Together with her travelling companion Helen, Kate had been living with an Iranian family, as guests of two brothers. The girls had met the two brothers on the bus as they drove into Tehran after arriving at the airport from India. Hamid and Rahmin were air traffic controllers coming off duty. A few days before this meeting Hamid had had an intense dream in which he had met a beautiful western girl, and the next morning he had drawn from memory the girl in his dream. Now sitting on the bus with her shinning eyes and open smile Hamid believed literally he had found the girl of his dreams. He fell completely in love with her. Hamid had invited the girls to their family home in the conservative south of Tehran, and they had stayed for a while, with Kate and Hamid entering into a secret relationship. But after several months of living in the same house with an extended family and the intensity of Hamid's feelings, it had all become too much for the girls. Kate's moving out had been painful for Hamid, even disastrous. The girls talked about him in hushed, slightly awed tones. Since Kate's departure, he had stayed in the house for weeks, hardly eating or speaking. Kate and Helen put Hamid's condition down to the fact that he was an Iranian, unused to the intimacy of western style relationships. When I talked to anyone about Hamid, I borrowed this explanation.

'He just wasn't used to our kind of relationships,' I would say, with authority.

During the first weeks of my relationship with Kate other

men from her recent past turned up. Tarik, an Iranian who had been living in the States for many years, had met the girls while teaching at their previous air force base. He arrived unannounced one evening in his beat-up VW Beetle. Helen met him at the door.

'Tarik! Hi, how are you? Come on in!'

Helen was warm and friendly, the kind of person always concerned that things were okay. Tarik came in.

'Tonight there is traditional Iranian music at my friend's restaurant,' I heard Tarik say; 'I would like to invite you. You are my guests.'

I came out with Kate from her room.

'Hi Tarik,' said Kate, and then to me, 'Ken this is Tarik.'

'Hello,' I said.

Tarik looked at me for a few seconds, 'Hello,' he said.

And we shook hands. Helen brightly filled the ensuing silence.

'Well guys! Shall we go?'

We started driving in a deadly silence into the city. On a dual carriage way Tarik suddenly swerved through a gap in the central divide, and drove head-on into the oncoming traffic. The windscreen was full of head lights, vehicles flashed past, their horns blaring, dropping an octave as they missed us.

'Tarik! Please don't do this. Please Tarik, don't do this,' begged Helen in the front.

I sat in the back with Kate, terrified. Tarik cut sharply back, crossing both lanes and pulling off at a right angle. We all got out, while he sat in silence, holding the steering wheel, staring madly at the blank wall of the road side buildings, all closed up behind steel roller shutters.

'Is he all right?' I asked concerned, not wanting to understand what was going on.

'Come on Ken ,' said Helen, pulling me away. 'It's okay, he's okay.

He's just upset. Just leave him alone.'

'But why? I mean, what a crazy thing to do!' I said as we walked back towards the apartment. 'He could have killed us.'

'He's pretty intense,' explained Helen, 'he's into Sufism.'

Another day a rather eccentric English man called Alastair turned up to say good-bye to Kate and Helen. He was on his way back to India. He wore baggy cords and a tatty sports jacket. He travelled with his luggage in an old pram. He had also been a teacher at the Airforce base where Kate and Helen had taught before moving house. He sat in the kitchen and chatted with Kate and Helen. I felt left out. I wanted Kate to tell him who I was. But she didn't, and I watched Alastair charm her as she laughed with delight at his Englishness. Later, when I asked Kate about Alastair, she told me what an extraordinary person he was, but nothing of what had been between them. Had they been lovers? I didn't ask her, I couldn't bear the answer. Kate seemed to cherish all these relationships and talked of Hamid, Tarik and Alastair as if they were dear old friends. She had scrapbooks and diaries filled with photos and mementoes, not only of the places she had been but also of the people she had known. As far as I was concerned they were her history. Now she was mine, there wasn't anyone else, not now, not ever.

I was living in a large, modern apartment on the outskirts of Tehran with Jess, my travelling companion. I had met him at art school where we were both taking an art foundation course. Neither of us had gone on to do a degree course afterwards. I hadn't even applied, I was through with educational institutions. They seemed only concerned with getting jobs, and I was hungry for Life. I wanted to know about the world I had been born in. I wanted to travel. In my bedroom I pinned up maps and planned journeys by drawing improbable lines across whole continents.

After our art student friends had gone to take their degrees at different art colleges around the country, Jess and I were left alone and we had become inseparable friends. During the summer we took LSD, and I watched the water in a pond unravel down to molecules. Cutting an orange in two I found I was unable to eat, it was too beautiful, almost sacred. Life seemed far too extraordinary to waste on a career. To earn some money I took a job delivering machine parts and toxic chemicals. I drove from one industrial waste land, peppered with desperate looking high-rise apartments, across brutal motorways to the next. The job suited me, letting me be on my own, not having to conform, seeing the real world where real people lived, and I liked being on the road.

One day I picked up a couple hitch-hiking. They were travellers, living out of small back packs, sleeping in churches, eating left-overs at service stations and doing Yoga in the mornings. They didn't smoke and were vegetarians. They'd been to India and were unlike any one else I had ever met. I brought them home to the village where I lived with my parents. We talked half the night about the places they had been, how they lived, what they believed in. After years of making travel plans for journeys that I wondered if I'd ever have the courage to begin, they showed it could be done. They told me about Yoga ashrams in India, the deserts of Afghanistan, the beaches in Thailand and also small but reassuring details like the cost of buses and hotels, how to carry my money and where to stay in Istanbul. As we talked, and they dismissed my hesitations, a door was thrown open and suddenly the future was in my grasp.

The next morning, after I had dropped my new friends back at the motorway, I drove to Rugby and dragged Jess out of bed to join me on a delivery to Dagenham.

'Come on, come on,' I called up to him, 'I've got something

important to tell you.'

Jess came down the stairs of the two-up, two-down, terraced house he lived in, tucking his shirt in. He was smaller than me, skinny, with shoulder length dark hair that fell over his eyes. He took my badgering with good humour. He began to lace his lovingly polished Doc Martin boots with such detailed perfection I nearly dragged him bodily from the house.

'For Christ's sake, Jess!' I begged, 'do them up in the van!'

As we drove along in the noisy cab, with Jess trying to adjust to being awake before noon, I was unable to hold back a second longer.

'Jess,' I declared, 'we're going to India!'

Jess was used to my enthusiasms. He was two years older and was by nature reserved. With his usual equanimity he smiled wryly and said,

'Oh yeah?'

Just before I met Kate, Jess's father died. We were sitting together cross legged on the balcony of our Tehran apartment when the post arrived. Jess went to get the letters and came back crying. I had never seen Jess cry. He had flown back to England for a month. I couldn't imagine going back. By then England felt like another world. I felt that if I went back I would lose all the freedom and happiness. It felt as if I would get sucked in to another reality and would never again have the courage to leave. Now, with Jess gone, I was on my own, it was a new experience, it felt more grown up, and I had met Kate.

The apartment had four large bedrooms, and we shared it with American Brad, a half Chinese, hash smoking traveller, and Annika, his slinky, Norwegian girlfriend. We had met them at the one hotel where all the travellers stayed when passing through Tehran. We had all been on our way back from India and we were all trying to get work teaching. We moved into the apartment during July, the hottest month in Tehran. The heat was so dry that when I hung my washing out on the flat concrete roof, the first item was dry before I had hung up the last. The apartment was unfurnished and uncarpeted and, as we only had the contents of our bags, we camped in the bare, hot rooms, sleeping on broken up cardboard boxes beneath the air-conditioning ducts. In the kitchen we prepared our food on the floor on old newspapers, cooking on a battered Primus stove that Jess and I had bought in Afghanistan.

Musavir, our landlord, lived in the apartment downstairs with his wife and three children. To the down-town agency which had let the place to Brad, we had been presented as Imperial Iranian Air Force language teachers. At first Musavir was clearly taken aback that we had no furniture. He had probably expected more conventional tenants. But Musavir was not a man to judge people by their furniture. He had been a bit of a radical when he was young, and so instead of mistrusting us, he turned up one afternoon, a few weeks after we had moved in, with foam mattresses, a table, chairs and gas cooker for the kitchen.

'You no more sleeping on boxes!' he told us with a great grin.

'This one no good,' he said pointing at our dented Afghani Primus stove, 'this one much better,' he said proudly patting the new gas stove.

He was right.

Musavir was a big man, open and friendly with a great sense of humour. He became like an uncle who decided we needed looking after. On his return from work, after changing into his traditional baggy pyjamas, he would often come upstairs to check on us.

'How are you today, Mr Ken?' he would demand, putting a thick arm around my shoulders, and casting an eye around the flat. Locked under his comradely grip, his arm as thick as my thigh, he would steer me around the rooms. Noticing an orange crate we had covered in a cloth as a table he laughed a booming laugh at our efforts.

'You make it one table!' he told me, man to man.

Brad found Musavir's way of coming up and checking on us irritating. He was rather tense despite smoking enormous quantities of hash.

'Why does he have to keep snooping around up here?' Brad complained.

But I liked Musavir. He was my first middle aged friend. He was cool.

A few days after Jess came back from England I discovered Kate and Helen were having problems where they were living. They shared their apartment with an English couple, both Air Force teachers. Unfortunately the man was a heroin addict, and every week his habit grew, and the more he took the more difficult it became to live with him. When he was high he acted, and looked, like a Russian count. He had a pointed goatee beard and curling moustache. He behaved with an air of disdain for the world. But when he hadn't enough to stay up, he became irrational and unpredictable. His girl friend, an innocent English Rose, fussed around him, apologising for him, cooking and cleaning for him, pretending things were going to get better. Kate and Helen could see they weren't, and they had decided to move out. I suggested that they come and live in our apartment and a few days later they moved in, bringing little more than a backpack each. I felt this move would finally bring Kate and me together. We would be a real couple living together. It was like getting married. At bed time on the first evening lost in my own happiness, I suggested that Helen stay with Jess. They were both a little shy but seemed to like each other and, as things worked out, fifteen years later they were still together.

Cocooned as we were in the two apartment building with a shared stairwell and one front door, Musavir and his family slowly became part of our lives. As in many traditional Islamic societies intimate social interaction was between extended family members only. Visiting friends would be treated as the rules decreed, men meeting men, women meeting women. But we transcended all these mores, we were young and easy going, and free from these social conditions. We had no family, no status, no religion and no one nationality. We treated them as friends, and there grew between us a warmth and closeness that touched all our lives. During the day Kate, Helen and Annika became regular visitors to the downstairs apartment with its big rooms free of all furniture except the beautiful carpets. There they sat and chatted with Suran, Musavir's shy and lovely wife and her three children. Suran's life was transformed by their arrival, and over the months we watched her become more self confident and out going. She started to learn English and the girls encouraged her to hold her own against Musavir.

'Why not make him do the washing up?' Annika asked, outrageously.

Suran would laugh a shy laugh at the suggestion and Musavir would happily defend his lazy ways.

Musavir did not object to this outside influence on his wife and family, he took it in his stride. He seemed to enjoy our bohemian life style. He would often invite us all down at the weekend for a large family meal, and afterwards bring out his opium smoking pipe. Musavir would first smoke himself, then slapping the carpet beside him say,

'Mr Ken! Beshin! Sit down!'

So I would go and sit by this great amiable, opium smoking uncle and he would pat my knee with his enormous hand and beam happily.

'Now you smoke!'

I would draw with the required strength, pulling the dangerous sweet hot smoke into my lungs until the pellet of opium was a black crisp, emptied of its narcotic content. The effects were strange and wonderful, I could lie if I wished with my eyes closed, and watch a passing display of Persian carpets which floated before my inner eye. I felt completely at peace. Musavir, like the bogey man at the school gates, was happy for any of us to smoke with him. Suran, however, made it clear she did not approve of Musavir giving us opium, particularly to the girls. Yet it was always a family event. We sat or lay around on the floor. The kids played and jumped on us, sometimes Jess and I entertained them by drawing cartoons. The girls chatted, and Suran supplied us all with endless glasses of black tea and bowls of smashed up rock sugar which was taken at a rate of a lump per mouthful of tea.

One morning, a month or so after Kate and Helen had moved into our apartment, I was called into my supervisor's office at the Air Force base.

'They want to see you over at, section 32,'

I looked blank.

'Don't you know what section 32 is?' he asked.

'I've never heard of it,' I replied.

'Well, it is Security,' he said, looking me in the eyes. Then added accusingly, 'Counter Espionage.'

'Why do they want to see me?' I asked, suddenly afraid.

He just shrugged and gave me a look that said whatever it was, he was sure I was guilty. I knew enough stories of Iran's hated secret police, the sinister sounding Savak, to be very anxious as I walked over for my 'interview'.

After a nail biting wait I was shown into an ordinary looking office. Behind the desk sat a sharply dressed air force officer who was reading papers from a file. I stood waiting. Finally he looked up and beckoned me to sit. After considering the document in front of him for a few moments, he asked me, 'Are you married?'

His question was obviously not an opening to polite conversation.

'No I am not married,' I answered.

He surveyed the document for a few moments longer.

'Do you have any intention to get married while you are employed by the Imperial Iranian Airforce?'

'No', I replied, 'I don't'.

'Then,' he said, 'you will sign this. '

He pushed a pre-written document across the desk. I read to my amazement a prewritten declaration of my non intent to get married. Without hesitation I signed it and pushed it back.

'Good,' he said with obvious pleasure.

He looked at me and said simply, 'you may go.'

As I walked back to the language department my relief and amusement were overshadowed by the realisation that I would have married Kate, if I had half a chance. It never occurred to me that Kate had left in her wake a jealous admirer in the secret police.

There was one other, more disturbing, occasion when I came face to face with the Savak. While down at the local shops one morning we had been befriended by an Iranian Bahai. He had latched onto us, followed us home and invited himself into our apartment. He proved to be dull company, but he hung around. We couldn't work out what he wanted. He had been there for ten minutes when there was a knock at the front door. I opened it to find myself faced with four gangsters dressed in an assortment of trench coats, polo necked pullovers, double-breasted suits and sporting cloth caps at rakish angles. Two of them casually held machine guns while a third had an automatic tucked into his trouser waistband. They introduced themselves as policemen.

'We want to see the Iranian man here,' they demanded.

There were three Iranians in the flat at that moment, and there were a few joints on the go, and probably enough hashish to put us all away for life. After a frantic attempt to hide the evidence of hashish possession we were left with the dilemma of which of our three guests was to go out. Bravely one friend, with a small history of dissent, went to the front door, but they spotted the Bahai.

'You,' they shouted in Farsi, 'Out!'

He went out looking terrified. We watched helplessly as they dragged him down the stairs and bundled him into the back of their car. We saw him a few days later, his face badly bruised. He was reluctant to speak to us. We asked him why he had been taken, and he gave us an unconvincing explanation about the police wanting information about what went on in our flat. In our innocence it did not occur to us that the police would beat people up because of their religious beliefs, and he was too afraid, or too ashamed, to enlighten us.

As autumn came the apartment became cold, especially the marble floor tiles. As before, Musavir arrived triumphantly with workmen who carpeted the entire apartment with cheap wall to wall carpets. We bought Aladdin paraffin stoves which gave a tiny source of heat in the large rooms. During the summer months the apartment had acquired homeliness with cotton wall hangings and rugs on the floors. We had inherited a beat-up cassette deck that played music which would come to remain forever a gateway to that time, filling me with unexpected joy and sorrow whenever I heard it.

By now Kate and Helen were getting towards the end of their contracts. They had arrived a month before Jess and me. This was fortunate for them because, just as we arrived, the short contracts were extended from six to nine months. This meant that if Kate was to leave Iran at the end of her contract, we would be separated for at least four months. This was bad news for me, because if I didn't see Kate for a day I was longing for the evening, and the thought of her being away for months filled me with fear. Kate was loving and kind, but she offered me no reassurance.

'You will be okay,' she told me.

'We can meet up in India,' I said.

'Maybe,' she replied, 'who knows what will happen?'

'Sure,' I lied, 'who knows what the future will bring?'

This was part of our philosophy, going with the flow, living freely within life's uncertainties. It was my problem if I couldn't handle it. She remained beautifully removed, floating through a sea of amazing people. I was one of them, but only if I could stay afloat. I wanted her to tell me I had landed the leading role but she wouldn't. I had to live in the present, the here and now, carry on the illusion and try not to think about the future.

The winter came to Tehran quite suddenly, changing within a few days from mild autumn weather to snow and ice. In the apartment condensation froze an inch thick on the bottoms of the metal framed windows. As Christmas drew near Kate seemed to relax into me. We cuddled up together under quilts during the morning. She was giving me what I wanted, just for Christmas. When the Christmas holiday came we drew together with our friends, and we were proud to have our own traditional festival. We decorated the apartment, bought a Christmas tree and gave each other cards. On Christmas day we cooked a big meal and invited our Iranian and western friends. We had become a big, easy going and happy family.

At the end of January Kate and Helen completed their contracts. They stayed at home during the day preparing to leave, packing possessions in boxes and sending them to the States. It was hard for me to leave and go to work. I wanted to be detached and cool, but I couldn't.

'I'll miss you so much,' I told her, unable to stop myself.

'I'll miss you too,' she said gently, 'I'll write.'

But she never said the things I longed to hear. I'll come back. We'll meet in India. I'll wait for you. I love you.

Before leaving for India Kate and Helen decided to make a trip around Iran. I managed to get leave for ten days so I could go with them. In early January the three of us boarded a twenty-four-hour bus to Bandar Abbas on the eastern end of Iran's Gulf coast. After spending a few days basking in the gulf coast warmth we travelled back north to the isolated desert city of Yazd. Yazd in January was bitterly cold. The single story mud buildings were bleak and desolate. All the roads and buildings seemed to be the same colourless, muddy brown. It was a frontier town, bordering on to the empty deserts and tribal lands of Afghanistan and Baluchistan. We got a room in a guest house that was full of nomads in from the desert to trade. Packed into rough rooms with mud floors they sat around the outer walls smoking from huge water hookahs, bundled up like Michelin men in their many layered long coats. They watched us with a detached curiosity. Although our room had a stove, it was so cold we had to get into bed and sit wrapped in blankets to stay warm. Later we went to the hammam, the traditional hot baths. There were individual bathing cubicles, each with a dressing area and shower. Kate said, quite casually, that she would share with Helen. It was a calculated act, a rejection of the intimacy we had shared. Even Helen was surprised, and urged Kate to share with me. I was grateful, loathing my weakness, unable to understand what motivated her.

Kate and Helen wanted to go to Shiraz, several hundred miles to the south west. They planned to visit another Iranian friend, a high-ranking officer from the Air Force. They would be staying at his house, and I was not invited. My ten days were soon to be up, and I knew I would have to return to Tehran alone. It was agreed that I would accompany them as far as Shiraz. There were no buses across the desert between Yazd and Shiraz, so we decided to hitchhike. We walked out of Yazd to where the small and seldom used road disappeared off into the desert. We waited for an hour, stamping our feet and blowing into our hands, before an oil tanker, streaked in mud caked oil, pulled up beside us with a great exhalation of air brakes.

'Shiraz miram?' we shouted up.

'Baleh! Yes!' replied the driver.

His mate climbed across into his side of the two seat cab and the three of us and our bags were squashed into the passenger seat. We drove through the frozen desert wastes chatting with the driver in shouted sentences. He took us to his home in a small village off the main road. They welcomed us with characteristic Iranian warmth, treating us like long lost relatives. Later in the afternoon, up in the mountains, he pulled his truck off the road and, while his mate made tea on a fire of twigs, he smoked a pipe of opium. Once we arrived in Shiraz we were back with all the hassles of a big city. The shouts, 'Hey Meester!' The streets that were alive with business, the push and shove of making money. I missed the solitude of Yazd with its empty, colourless streets, the uncomplicated nomadic people and the surrounding deserts. The cold, windy emptiness had been strangely comforting. Now I felt defenceless, afraid.

When the moment came for me to part with Kate I feigned an easy-going attitude. I knew she was leaving me, not just physically but emotionally. She made it clear by how she talked of the future, ever vague, always uncommitted, trying to warn me off. But I hoped against desperate hope that if I could just be cool enough, detached enough, I might finally, in the last moments, win her heart. I gave her a hug and a wave, and walked alone back to the cheap hotel where the three of us had been staying. Without Kate the room seemed different. The dirty orange curtains, the tatty modern furniture and grubby walls became sordid, careless; a compassionless, transient world that cared nothing if I lived or died. I was completely alone for the first time in my adult life. A wave of cold desolation engulfed me, and for the first time for many years I began to cry.

A week later, when Kate and Helen returned to Tehran, they began their final preparations to leave. Kate was friendly, but now she kept a distance. Like the stuff she had packed away in her boxes, I was already memories, just one of the many interesting features from her life in Iran. I could not tell her of my breaking heart; that wouldn't be cool. It would not be the detached and together person I believed I must become. It might force her to say the things I did not want her to say. That she was leaving me, that it was over. The last morning came, then the last hour and finally we were standing in the apartment hallway where we had agreed to part. We had planned it; feeling it would be better this way. It was just like the beginning of term at boarding school, my mother unnaturally bright, suddenly a cheerful stranger, standing on the grey stone steps, the agreed place, like the hall in the apartment. A small boy in flannel trousers, trying not to cry, nor beg them not to leave, being a brave boy. Kate and I hugged and kissed and she turned and walked away down the stairs. Back in my room, emptied of her belongings, I paced blindly around unable to believe or accept what was happening. Then I let out a great tear-filled cry and ran from the room out on to the street, I was running to stop her, down the road to the empty corner where her taxi had been waiting. One last moment, one more touch. In my head I was shouting, begging, 'Don't go! Don't go! Don't go! Oh God, please, please, let her stay.'

Within a week of Kate leaving I began to think about following her. Once I allowed this thought some space it began to
take hold, and the more I thought about it, the more I felt I had
to do it. Finally, with the arrival of a national holiday that
would extend the finishing date of my contract yet another
unbearable two weeks, I decided to follow Kate to India. I
would lose the money held back from the five week training
period, and my current month's pay. Altogether this was a con-
siderable amount, the bulk of what I had hoped to save from
my stay in Iran. But I couldn't weigh money in the balance
against my desire to see Kate. What was money compared to
love? When I said this to Jess it sounded foolish, but I argued
my position with intensity, I didn't want to accept any of the
possibilities doing nothing entailed. Jess accepted my decision
to go, he had also parted with Helen and was missing her. But
he had equanimity, I had none.

Musavir was astonished and offered his blunt advice unhesi-
tatingly.

'Mr Ken ! You leave it this one. You take it another one!'

I tried to explain to him how much I loved Kate, and I was
shocked when Musavir only slapped his thigh in disbelief,
laughed at my words and shook his head.

'Mr Ken ,' he said with concern, while tapping his temple
with one finger, 'you one hundred percent crazy... '

But it was too late. The decision was made. My sadness and
longing were replaced by an excited fear. I knew what I was
doing was crazy, but I couldn't stop myself. Having said Kate
meant more to me than money, how could I change my mind?
I would also be parting from Jess. It was not that I wanted to,
but I felt it was time to grow up, to be alone.

'I'll see you in India,' I joked with him, half serious, half
aware of the implications. 'Either I'll be with Kate, or I'll be
living as a Yogi under a tree.'

As it was the beginning of a national holiday every form of public transport out of Tehran was fully booked, but I managed to get an internal flight to Mahshad on the eastern border with Afghanistan. I said good-bye to everyone at the flat. My Iranian friends, Musavir and Suran gave me black and white photos of themselves, an Iranian custom, with messages written on the back.

'To one of my best friend,' wrote one, 'I wish you success in your life.'

I travelled back overland. I was playing the role I had prepared for Kate. I was wearing the dark blue velvet pyjama trousers gathered at the ankle, Aladdin style, that she had said looked beautiful. I wore a long white Indian cotton shirt and my Afghani embroidered nomad's waistcoat. I had exchanged my kit bag for two hand-woven shoulder bags which were too heavy and cut into my shoulders, but they looked good. I had become an actor in a role I did not understand, a self created drama with a cast of one. I had written to Kate just before I left Iran to say I was coming. I asked her to leave me a note at Poste Restante in New Delhi saying where I could find her. I arrived in New Delhi after seven days hard travelling; it was a Saturday afternoon and the Post Office was shut until Monday. That evening I chatted to an Australian at the guest house where I was staying. I told him how I was on my way to join up with my girlfriend, and proudly I showed him a photo of Kate.

'Hey,' he said looking at the picture, 'I met her in Varanasi, she was together with some English bloke, he had all his gear in a pram.'

A dreadful numbness soaked through me filling my veins with liquid wood. 'How do you know they were together?' I asked, 'like that.'

'It was pretty obvious,' he said, casually, but then seeing the look on my face added kindly, 'never mind Mate. You win some, you lose some.'

Monday morning came. After breakfast I walked to the Post Office to collect my mail from Poste Restante. There was only one letter, the hand writing was Kate's. I read it standing on the Post Office steps. She explained her need to be alone, how she needed to have some space, how she had never meant to hurt me and that she wished me well. The letter was only true in one place and that was on the back. There, all the words and explanations were exposed; there was no senders address. I could have taken a taxi to Delhi Airport and been back for work the next day, but the humiliation was too great, I could not go back.

The Australian had said Kate was heading up to Kathmandu from Varanasi. So, instead of going back, I went to the office of the Nepalese bus service to Kathmandu. It was a two-day journey with a one night stop-over in Pokhara, a village in western Nepal. The next morning at 4 a.m. I left Delhi and by the evening I was in Pokhara, walking along a quiet green lane with snow-capped mountains in the distance. Ahead I saw two girls walking towards me, and with a mixture of joy and horror I realised they were Kate and Helen. I felt sick and dizzy. We all hugged and exchanged absurd pleasantries. I told them how I had heard they were in Kathmandu. I acted like meeting them was   just some happy coincidence and I asked them where they were going. They were on the same bus journey, with the same company, only going the other way. Then they told me they were on their way back to Iran. I was functioning but not much more, I showed no emotion, playing out the role I had prepared. 'Hey, nice to see you. Me? I'm cool. Look, no big scene, no tears, no fuss.' I could not break out of this act. The last time I'd openly wept, shown my feelings she'd left me. I wasn't going to do it twice. This was my only chance. One last shot. I'd be cool, detached, she might still have a change of heart, impressed by my equanimity, my detachment. 'Come back with us,' she might say.

Kate stayed the night with me but I was ill with diarrhoea. She allowed me to make love to her, but with terrible shits and the tension it didn't work. We lay uncomfortably on the hard planks of the crude bed and made small talk, telling lies. The next morning I was still cool, I made no scene. I waved them off as their bus pulled out, but being cool had not worked and she was leaving. Then she was gone, and I was alone, left only with my act. I wandered around for the rest of the day surrounded by the beautiful, but meaningless scenery. I kept finding my jaw was aching and my teeth hurting because they were clenched so tight. I had to keep remembering to unclench them. In my head the words of the Bob Dylan song Highway 61 played like a tape loop in my mind. When I awoke in the middle of the night, my jaw aching, the words were still there, running round and round and round.

'God said to Abraham, 'Kill me your son...'

Chapter 2

ENGLAND 1979

'Going to India eh?' asked the dentist as he filled more of my teeth, 'Why, what's in India?'

Why? Who knew why anyone was doing anything?

'I'm going to see the south,' I replied and was amazed at how this to me meaningless answer was accepted as rational. I was back in England after three years travelling. After my journey to India to be reunited with Kate, I had gone to Japan. I had landed at Haneda international airport just four weeks after leaving Iran, and taken a crowded commuter train into Tokyo city. I was still dressed in my velvet Arabian nomadic kit; pyjamas gathered at the ankle, tatty velvet waistcoat embroidered with gold and the big, uncomfortable shoulder bags. School girls tittered behind their uplifted hands while hundreds of identically suited Japanese men pretended not to notice me. At the guest house I tore off these clothes and went to the nearest clothes shop. I blindly bought the first clothes I saw; a pair of slightly furry, grey trousers, a white shirt and an off grey tie. Back in my tatami-floored cubicle of a room I completed the new identity by shaving off my beard. I looked at myself in the mirror, the cool hippie traveller had gone. Instead of the beautiful person Kate had conjured up there was a stranger, a nerdy head boy, an idiotic accounting clerk. I was afraid it was the real me.

During a year in Japan I put myself back together. I taught English, made friends, drank until my kidneys hurt and got used to being alone. I left Japan on a cargo ship heading south to Bangkok. I travelled down through south east Asia to Australia. I spent a year hitching around Australia feeling more and more disconnected and directionless. I took to reading Krishnamurti books, practising Yoga and eating strange diets of raw food. I ended up at a Yoga Ashram north of Sydney at the end of a track deep in the forest. The ashram was run by a young Indian Swami called Bhaktiananda. He wore orange robes and had the shaven head of a sanyassin, a renunciate. Bhaktiananda had been selected by his Guru, Swami Rajananda, to come to Australia and establish an ashram. He was a Hindu missionary. Rajananda was a famous Yoga guru in India who could count Indira Ghandi among his many rich and influential pupils.

The Ashram was well established and there were many resident Australian sanyassins. They had Hindu names, but for the most part were referred to only as Swami, a title of respect. The Swamis and nuns lived an austere life style. They were celibate, owned no possessions and lived only by offerings. Their main work outside the ashram was to teach Yoga. I found I was quickly at ease with the simple life style of the ashram; sitting and sleeping on the floor, eating Indian vegetarian food, adopting the language and having conversations about the spiritual quest. What I had never seen before was the Guru devotion. Bhaktiananda was young, good looking and accepted all the adulation with ease. He had come empty-handed to Australia a few years earlier, an envoy sent by Rajananda, but had quickly acquired an entire following of his own. Now he wore a silver 'OM' symbol on a chain around his neck, and had bought, or been given, a huge car, which was bright orange, to match his robes. The devotional attitude made me uncomfortable. Especially as I just could not feel any devotion for Bhaktiananda at all. I found it disturbing to see how rational and intelligent people suddenly became subservient and creeping when he appeared. They would hang on his every word, however banal, and be made happy if he merely noticed their existence. There was a creepy one-upman-ship amongst the residents which Bhaktiananda played on. I noticed too how the children who lived at the ashram were infected by it. I overheard one child humiliating another, 'I heard Bhaktiananda say your mum has got a lot of negative karma.'

Bhaktiananda lived in a small house at the top of the valley with his attendant, a young and strikingly pretty Australian nun who remained rather aloof from the other ashramites. In a community where receiving a smile from the Guru would make someone's day, being his personal attendant was high status indeed. I wondered at these two celibates sharing a house, but kept my blasphemous thoughts to myself.

One sunny afternoon I was watching some swamis and ashramites playing volley ball. Bhaktiananda was playing too, it was his favourite game. As I watched a member of Bhaktianada's team, a swami, missed a rather easy shot losing the game. Bhaktiananda slowly walked over to him and picked up the ball. He held it out on the palm of his left hand towards the failed player as if offering it to him. Everyone waited and watched. Then, with a blow from his right fist, Bhaktiananda punched the ball straight into his team mate's face. The blow sent the swami staggering backwards clutching his face with a cry of pain. Bhaktiananda turned away and carried on as if nothing had happened and everyone followed suit. I turned, wide eyed, to a swami standing beside me.

'Did you see that?' I asked, incredulously.

He turned to me with soft and untroubled eyes and replied, 'he must have needed it.'

The Yoga teachings at the ashram put a great emphasis on physical purity. The ashram literature described a wide range of ancient Yogic methods for cleaning out the bodily tubes, pipes and organs. In fact, there hardly seemed to be an orifice or organ in the body that did not require flushing, unblocking or purifying. The techniques for internal cleaning were pretty bizarre. They included such skills as the ability to suck water up one's bottom and expel it, or to pour water into one nostril, and expel it out of the other. Another technique was to drink water over a long period and, along with yoga exercises, continue until one was passing it clean, through the bowels. There was a sense that the body was something unclean, and that unhappiness, impurity of mind, was a result of the impure body.

I decided my unwashed innards must be completely filthy, all gunged up with accumulated muck. I saw myself like one long kitchen sink U bend, and I thought Real Happiness was surely impossible with such innards. So I began to practice what was definitely the most popular purification technique at the ashram. This was done first thing in the morning. It was simple. Drink two litres of warm salty water and then vomit it back up. According to the books this aquatic bulimia had many benefits, including the prevention of over acidity, the removal of coughs and sore throats, the relieving of asthma and a general healthy stimulation of the abdominal organs. In fact after a couple of months it made me ill. Not long after leaving the ashram my entire oesophagus went on strike, I couldn't swallow for days and was left plagued by acidic indigestion.

I was disillusioned. I had been on the road for three years, but I was not sure why anymore. In fact why anyone did anything seemed a mystery. I longed for a reason to be. I longed for peace and happiness. So I left Australia and returned to England intending to study for a degree in fine art. I thought perhaps I could pick up on the life I had left in England three years before. I arrived back in March, and the academic year began in the autumn. My father and brother were about to depart to France with a twenty four passenger hotel barge. A few weeks into the season my father called and offered me a job. So I spent the summer as a deck hand. I lusted after the stewardesses, drank beer, ate meat, put on weight and felt as if I had rejoined the world.

Once the season was over I returned again to my parents home. It was November, the house was empty, and it was raining. I drove to Warwick where I hoped to study, to see about a place to live. In the rain sodden half light my motiveless plans and hopes dissolved into the black glistening roads. I drove back to the safe solitude of my parents' house. At the local library I searched the travel section, returning home with Heinrich Harrier and Wilfred Thessinger. With my feet toasting over an electric fire I escaped into the empty quarter of Arabia and across the plains of Tibet. I began to think about returning to India.

Jess was back in Rugby. He and Helen had been married in the summer. They were working for the post office, rising at five and walking the streets with enormous bags of mail. They intended to save up then to go to India for a year. American Brad and Norwegian Annika from the flat in Tehran arrived unannounced, just back from India. Brad had bought a huge piece of hash through customs, and narrowly escaped several close brushes with the Rugby drug squad. We sat around on the floor at Jess and Helen's, smoked dope and talked of old times. Jess told us stories of the revolution and how our Iranian friends had come round with their Kalashnikovs to smoke joints before going onto the streets to fight. He told us how quickly the euphoria of potential freedom had been overshadowed by the fundamentalists. He told us how the grocery shop owner at the corner of our street where we bought our veggies and milk, who had a few shelves of beer and spirits, found his ten year old son murdered on his door step, with a note denouncing him as corrupt. Yet through all this the last few at the flat had kept on teaching English to private students, climbing the previous nights barricades and detouring round gun battles to get to work.

Brad and Annika wanted to get married, so we booked them in at the Registry office. We decorated the hotel barge mini bus with ribbons and flowers, Iranian style, and drove around Rugby wildly blowing the horn. An Iranian custom that was not well received in Rugby town centre. Then Kate came over from the States. She had changed in the last two years. She had become involved in spiritualism and the occult. She told me of wizards she knew who could see people's previous incarnations in mirrors, of spirits and powers. But she did not look well or happy. She seemed to have lost her radiant beauty. Her once shining eyes now seemed blank, staring, with dark shadows beneath them. She had come to England to see someone closely connected with the Seth phenomenon. Seth was the name of a spirit being who had, through a medium, transmitted the contents of several very successful books. We went to London together, Kate wanted to see her Seth connection and I was going to get a flight to India. She would not let me accompany her to the meeting, telling me I was too negative about Seth, which I was.

We stayed with Bernard and Barbara, a couple who were old friends of Kate and Helen's from their early days in India. They were squatting in the deserted apartment where Bernard had grown up. The rooms were bare and there was no electricity. One evening, by candle light, sitting around the fire, I picked up a book. It was called, 'The Wheel of Dharma.'

'Bernard,' I asked, 'what does Dharma mean?'

'What does Dharma mean?' he asked, laughing as if I had cracked some witty joke, 'that's a good question.'

I talked to Barbara about India and she promised to write

and give me addresses of places to visit.

Kate was due to fly back to America, to her boyfriend. I had found it strange to be with her again. I was not attracted to the occult, and we had little in common but the past. We slept together for the two weeks she was in England. It just seemed the natural thing to do. It was an act of forgiveness, apology and completion. With the old ghosts laid to rest I saw her off at a tube station, and then hitch hiked alone back up the M1 to Rugby. Just before I left for India, I received a letter from Barbara. She gave me directions to a Japanese Buddhist temple in Bombay where I might be able to stay. She also mentioned a teacher called Nisargadatta who lived in Bombay. Visiting him was, 'worth a few trips round India,' and a teacher called Goenka who taught at Dharmagiri near the town of Igatpuri, just to the north of Bombay. With its sense of purpose, her letter helped me on my journey. I would go and stay at a Japanese Buddhist Temple. At least it was a direction to take out of the airport.

The night before I left, I threw the **I Ching**. I got the last chapter in the book, Before Completion. *'This hexagram,'* said the **I Ching**, *'indicates a time when the transition from disorder to order is not yet completed. The successful change is indeed prepared for, however things are not yet in their right places....'* From the following pages I read a warning and a prediction, *'...if the young and inexperienced fox rushes ahead where the ice is thin and it breaks before he has completed his crossing, then there is nothing that would further.... but if the crossing is successfully completed then, after three years, great realms will be rewarded..... '*

There were three other back packer tourists on the Iraqi Airways flight to Bombay. Our flight arrived, the way cheap flights do, very late at night, and we took a taxi together into the city. The taxi went from one full and dingy hotel to the next full dingy hotel. Groups of dangerous looking young men down back alleys playing cards looked at us with hostility as we struggled past. I felt we were too big and too clean, we were the rich west intruding into their privacy. The driver was doing his best, but with each rejection he became more worried, faced with the possibility of having us stuck in his taxi the whole night. Finally he offered to take us to a railway station where we could wait safely until dawn. As we got out of the taxi in front of the station, a bottle of duty-free whiskey slipped from someone's bag and smashed on the road. The pavement dwellers watched impassively as the whiskey leaked from the box like expensive blood and ran away into the gutter.

The station waiting rooms were as full as the hotels We spread out newspapers on the platform and tried to get some sleep. Dotted along the platform were what looked like heaps of rags, although when a train arrived these heaps turned out to be coolies and vendors. The arrival of a train was dramatic, with the ancient locomotives hissing and steaming past our makeshift camp, a wall of moving wet steel, close enough to touch. For a few minutes the station came alive with vendors and coolies touting for customers. Then a distant whistle, slamming doors, shouting voices and the train pulled out. Within moments the restless, dimly lit quiet returned. At dawn I shouldered my backpack and walked out into the cool first light. Bombay looked like a city after the holocaust. The buildings were black with mould as if the concrete and stone were rotting away. The streets had mounds of ancient rubbish at their edges where mangy dogs sniffed, searching for food. The larger streets were already busy with people on their way to work; men in white shirts and ties, the women in elegant saris. They formed long and orderly queues at the bus stops. They looked startlingly clean against the filthy streets. The roads were still quite quiet except for bicycles and battered buses.

The sun, now just above the roof tops, was already hot. I joined a bus queue.

The Japanese Temple was a heavily built stone building, a sort of Victorian version of a Hindu temple, set back from the road and hemmed in by city buildings. I left my shoes and bag at the door, and entered a spotlessly clean hall. At the far end was a big mural of the Buddha lying down looking very relaxed. In front of the mural were offerings and altars. To one side a young Japanese monk sat before a single drum, the size of a French wine vat, beating an unceasing intense rhythm. I sat down with the few other devotees and waited. After a few minutes the monk stopped drumming and went to the front of the temple. He knelt formally and beckoned me to join him. We knelt Japanese style facing each other. He bowed to me and I bowed back.

'This is Buddhist Temple,' he told me, 'you may come and visit here when ever you wish.'

'Thank you,' I replied, then taking a breath continued, 'actually I was hoping I might be able to stay here. . . . . '

The young monk paused for a few moments, 'Very sorry,' he said, 'but Abbot is away and this is month of fasting.'

I stood on the temple steps and wondered what to do next. The whole Indian sub continent seemed spread out in front of me, and yet I still had no idea why I was there. With the Buddha smiling at my back I decided, like thousands of other young western tourists, to go to Goa.

At the Bombay docks ferry terminal I sat for the whole day in a slowly filling waiting hall. There was an easy calm, a sense of time measured in days rather than hours and minutes. The hall was full by the late afternoon when the boarding gates opened. Then the laid-back calm was instantly transformed into chaos. Families frantically gathered their belongings and ran towards the open doors carrying their children. The clamour of shouted directions between friends and relatives added to the general hysteria. I stumbled, pushed and was pulled along with the crowd. We squeezed up the gang plank and burst over the decks. Immediately everyone began to stake out territories. Vast areas were snapped up in the unfurling of a large family rug. I pulled my frayed, lime green towel from my bag, it was the one I'd had at boarding school, it even had my name tag still hanging determinedly on in one corner. I staked a rather pathetic square, just big enough for me to sit on. The deck made the underside of the towel instantly filthy.

Three heavily tanned Italian travellers had made camp near by. They were sitting cross legged on a big Indian rug. They had bare feet and wore silver bangles and head scarves. Their faces were expressionlessly detached. They seemed to be travelling out of bags only slightly larger than my wash bag. One of them, very coolly, was rolling a joint. I made it very uncoolly clear I would like to share it, by grinning stupidly at them. After they had all smoked, one of them leaned over and, with a slight movement of his eyebrows, passed the joint over. I took several long pulls, then a few more and passed it back, trying all the while to look cool. It was strong stuff. As the chemicals flowed into my brain the hash swept away my tenuous connections with the past, my reference points, the illusory identity to which I hung, and I found myself catapulted, full on, into the vivid, colourful, raging, intensity of India, and paranoia. I got up and stood by the ship's railings and watched the dockers casting off. Their faces scared me, crazy, wizard faces with black, glinting eyes beneath flowing turbans. I had woken from a dream, but where the dream had been relatively safe, reality was terrifying. I felt like a passenger in a body and mind that took me to strange places and did strange things. I got out my drawing pad and drew a big Indian mother sitting impassively opposite in her white sari. It helped me through the fear, it brought back the order. Me in here, mother out there.

By the time I landed in Panjim, the capital of Goa, twelve hours later, I had slept off the hash and was struggling with the realisation that I was half way down the Indian subcontinent with, as far as I could make out, no reason to be there at all. I could hardly talk with other travellers. All I wanted to ask was, 'Why are you here? What on earth are we all doing? What is the point of it all?'

I caught a bus to the beach. It stopped in a square surrounded by stalls, at the edge of a village, in the shade of coconut palms. I was quickly picked up by a small boy who offered to take me to 'cheap room'. The room was dark, dirty and not particularly cheap. I agreed to stay because I couldn't face the hassles involved in refusing. I left my bag, and wandered off through the village towards the beach. The road was lined with shops selling clothes and handicrafts, and tea shops. From the tea shops rock music wafted out and scantily clad, beautiful people, sat smoking hashish and drinking tea. It was like a hippie Costa del Sol. Down on the beach a vast orange disc of a sun sank into a shimmering golden ocean as meaningless as a red coin slipping into a distant golden slot.

Sitting on the sand, still warm from the afternoon sun, with a cool breeze blowing in off the sea, I was filled with desolation and loss. But of what, I no longer knew. To fill the emptiness I made a fantasy. I would try to find a place to live, somewhere along the coast away from the commercial beaches. I would get a little house amongst the palms, just back from the beach. I would live there for a while, painting, being peaceful. I pictured my self doing yoga on the veranda in the early morning, strolling down between the palms for an early morning swim. It was a good fantasy, so good in fact I could hardly wait for it to begin.

The next morning I hurriedly dressed in the clothes from my

previous travels in Iran and Afghanistan. I shouldered my rucksack and set off up the beach. I walked its length then climbed the headland at the end. The sun was climbing in the sky and was hot on my back, so I stopped and tied a long cotton scarf around my head as a turban. The thorny bushes caught my voluminous baggy Afghan trousers. I was hot and flustered. My cheap rucksack, over-laden, cut into my lower back chafing the skin raw. On the far side of the headland the path descended steeply. I half stumbled, half ran the last fifteen feet exploding out through the undergrowth onto the sand, my baggy clothes flapping, looking like a demented Afghan Muhajadeen. I had arrived at Anjuna beach, probably the hippest place on earth. Languid, naked, beautiful people lay here and there on the perfect white sand. They watched me with detached interest as I struggled past as if I were seeking a mislaid rocket launcher.

Behind the beach I found the place of my fantasy, small cottages, shaded by palms, with whitewashed walls and red tiled roofs. Many had flowers growing in pots around the windows. In the doorway of one cottage, wearing only a coloured sarong, a man was standing. His body was a deep nutty brown, and his long hair was tied back in a pony tail. I asked him if there were any rooms available. He mused in a friendly way, but said he didn't think so, not at the moment. He suggested I live on the beach for a while, maybe something would come up in a few weeks. I saw myself sitting on my little green towel. What would I do all day? I hadn't come six thousand miles to sunbathe.

I returned to my dark, mosquito infested room. For five days I hung around the beach side tea shops drinking endless, expensive soft drinks. Finally on the fifth day I decided, rather desperately after my third bottle of Mangola juice, to walk from Goa south to Kerala, down the western coast of India.

The fantasy took hold like the room amongst the palms. I saw myself staying with villagers, a wandering yogi, experiencing the real India. I told a soft drink acquaintance about my plan. He was sceptical; he had travelled that way by bus. He said it was pretty desolate, miles of scrubby woodland and the roads were busy with traffic. His words made me afraid, but I did not give up on the idea. So it would be hard, I reasoned, but it would be a real experience, and anything had to be better than this meaningless limbo.

I went to Panjim town, found a hotel room and began to prepare for my epic journey. First, in order to lighten my load I sent off, to Poste Restante Calcutta, a distant destination in an even greater fantasy, all my warm clothes, including my jeans, sleeping bag and shoes. My silver flute I sent back to England, writing 'silver flute' on the contents label, realising an hour later, with yet another wave of despair, that it would now almost certainly be stolen in the post. While at the post office, ridding myself of my most essential and practical clothing and equipment, I struck up a conversation with another traveller. He told me he had just come from a meditation course at Igatpuri, north of Bombay, with a teacher called Goenka. I remembered the name from Barbara's letter. He told me the course was ten days long and in total silence. Apart from breaks for eating and resting, there was silent, sitting meditation from 4.30 in the morning until 9 at night. As he spoke I knew I had to go, I didn't want to walk to Kerala, I wanted to find the source of the haunting emptiness I felt inside, and if I could find it anywhere, then surely, I could find the answer in ten days of silent meditation.

'Is there another course?' I asked him, 'can I go there?'

'I think Goenka is teaching one more course this winter,' he told me, 'it starts in two days. You could just make it if you can catch the ship leaving for Bombay tonight.'

Chapter 3

I arrived in Igatpuri the next day. I checked into the only hotel in town, a rambling colonial style bungalow. It was full of young travellers gathering for the meditation course. I wandered around the hotel garden feeling rather shy. At one end of the long veranda a girl was sitting reading a book about Tibetan religious art. She had a long, thick mane of hair and sat with a very straight back. She looked very still. I began a conversation with her. She answered my questions kindly, but kept aloof, with sufficient repressed sensuality to make me desire her madly. She was from Sweden and her name was Eva. I asked her about the meditation course. It turned out it was her first meditation course too.

'Ten days is quite a long time not to speak,' I said, instantly wishing I hadn't.

'I don't think that it will be very difficult.' she replied softly, in her sing song accent.

'Well, no, of course, not actually difficult,' I blustered, 'but, er, unusual...'

'Perhaps....' she smiled.

She had also been an art student so we talked for a while about drawing and painting. She seemed to radiate sexual availability and simultaneously, total aloofness. I was irresistibly drawn to this catastrophic mix.

In one corner of the garden I joined a cluster of travellers. Most were newcomers like me. Some were easy going, like tourists about to try a new experience, others looked more serious. One, called Klaus, a German, looked pretty paranoid, his leg kept twitching and his clothes were dirty. He looked like a junkie. A beautiful young German girl sat with him, a protective angel. One of the group had sat several Goenka courses before. His name was Laurie and he was being questioned by the others about the course. There was something very up front about him. Nervously smoking cheap Indian cigarettes, he was enjoying being the centre of attention.

'You still smoke cigarettes,' I said, as if this fact discredited his meditation practice.

'Well', he replied cuttingly, 'there's no point in pretending you are more together than you are.'

His words touched a nerve. My whole life seemed to be pretending to be more together than I was. That was all I had. I couldn't stop pretending, it was inconceivable, I would just fall to bits. Laurie attracted me by being openly uncool and untogether, yet at the same time the conversation around him was lively, he listened and responded to what people said. There was an intensity about him that drew me, but also slightly frightened me. I felt as if at any moment my bluff could be called. Later in the day I came upon Laurie involved in an animated discussion with Eva. She was laughing with delight at something he was saying, and she looked beautiful. I felt a pang of jealousy.

It was a relief when the next afternoon we all trooped up to the meditation centre on the hill above the village. At least during the silent meditation course, with men and women segregated, Eva would be safe from possible seduction by Laurie. A large sign at the entrance proclaimed, Vipassana International Academy. I had expected something more ashram like. After all, who went to an academy to learn meditation? We passed the watchman's hut and walked up to the long low buildings. Tables had been set up outside for enrolment on to the course. They were manned by Indians and westerners. The westerners all looked very clean-cut, dressed in bank clerk shirts and plain, south-east Asian style lungis. Beards and long hair were definitely not in vogue. There were coloured forms in heaps on the tables for the different categories of student. New or old, male or female. I was given a pale green one, as I was a new male. I was a bit surprised by the detail the form went into. Father's name? Father's profession? Age? Livelihood? How did you hear about Vipassana meditation? Previous meditation experience? Medical history both mental and physical.... ? Some of the more bohemian travellers did not like the forms at all.

'Hey!' said one ragged Frenchman, angrily waving his green form, 'what is all zis shit?'

As the evening drew in we began to gather outside the meditation hall. There were several hundred people, mostly Indians but also westerners. The men were on one side, the women on the other. People talked little, waiting for silence to begin. The sun was setting beyond the meditation hall. The landscape around us was unearthly. Ancient cliffs eroded into pinnacles were silhouetted by the setting sun, bats flitted through the half light, and the whistles of stream trains at Igatpuri station wailed mournfully echoing around the cliffs.

A lungi clad westerner carrying a clipboard appeared from the entrance of the meditation hall. He read out the names of old students, noticeable by their serious look, waiting slightly apart. They all seemed to have big, light-weight shawls, giving them a slightly monkish look. I soon realised these shawls were a very useful item when sitting cross-legged for long periods. A sort of private tent to maintain heat or cold, and defend against mosquitoes. They entered the hall as their names were called, getting to sit on the better cushions at the front. Once all the old students had been called in, the new student rabble was allowed to enter. It was pretty undignified. We burst into the hall grabbing frantically at the ever decreasing heap of cushions at the back. I found myself with an eighteen inch square of what felt like one inch thick horsehair.

Once we had all settled down Goenka, our teacher, entered. He wore the same style of shirt and Burmese lungi worn by his western followers. He settled himself on the dais at the front with his wife beside him. She was to remain there throughout the course, unspeaking and unmoving. He looked around the hall slowly, impassively, then seemingly satisfied began to speak.

'You have all gathered here to practise the Buddha Dharma, the eight fold noble path as taught by Gotama the Buddha.'

His voice was very deep and resonant.

'And what is this eight fold path? It is divided into three parts. First, Sila, which means morality. Second, Samadhi, which means concentration of mind, and lastly, Panna, which means wisdom or insight.'

My bottom was already beginning to go numb, and my ankles hurt on the thin rug over the concrete floor.

'The new students will be practising Sila, morality, by observing the five precepts, while the old students will observe eight precepts. These precepts are basic rules of behaviour common to all religions. They are: not to kill or harm any living being, not to steal or take that which is not freely given, not to tell lies, which as you will be in complete silence should not be difficult,' he paused for a few polite giggles, 'not to commit sexual misconduct, which means, for the duration of the course, refraining from all sexual activity, and lastly to refrain from the use of any intoxicants. This rule applies to all drugs except those you require for a medical condition. Those are the five precepts for the new students.'

An Indian gentleman next to me nodded in pious agreement.

'For the old students there are a further three precepts: not to sleep on high and luxurious beds, not a problem here,' another pause for a ripple of laughter, 'not to sing or dance, and lastly, not to eat any food after midday. Your main meal will be served at eleven thirty in the morning. At 5 pm the new students will receive tea and a piece of fruit, the old students, however, will receive only lemon water.' Goenka paused. 'We will now take these precepts formally in Pali, the ancient language of the Buddha. I will chant the precepts in Pali and you repeat them after me.'

So I began to chant, in undoubtedly incomprehensible Pali, the five precepts.

Once this was finished Goenka continued.

'You now are established in Sila. This is the base from which you can develop Samadhi. Without this base being firm you cannot develop the stillness of mind required for Samadhi.'

My leg began to itch, and I looked down in time to see a bloated mosquito flying heavily away.

'To begin to develop concentration or Samadhi,' Goenka was saying, 'we need an object to concentrate on. The object of meditation the Buddha recommended was the breath. Life starts with a breath and finishes with a breath. The breath is closely associated with our mental state, the quieter we are the subtler it becomes.'

The hall became noticeably full of unnecessarily noisy inhalation and exhalation.

'In order to develop one pointedness of mind we will observe the breath in one place, that place will be the entrance to the nostrils. We will observe the sensation of the breath flowing over this part of the body, as it comes in and as it goes out.'

I tried to feel the breath at my nostrils. It was easy.

'At first you will find the mind wanders away. That is the nature of the mind. When you notice that the mind has wandered just gently bring it back, to the in-flow and out-flow of breath. Do not be disheartened, this is not easy. You are trying to break the habit of a life time. The Buddha said it is easier to tame a wild elephant than it is to tame the mind. So you will have to work hard and remember, no one else can do this work for you.' he paused, 'let us now meditate together.'

So I began to meditate, watching the breath, feeling the intense discomfort of sitting on the floor, my mind wandering away after every second breath. Every once in a while Goenka helped us along, his words suddenly filling the silence, bringing my attention back.

'...observing the natural flow of breath. Not trying to change or alter, just seeing the breath as it is. As it comes in and as it goes out. At the entrance of the nostrils and above the upper lip.'

I observed and there it was, as clear as day, a distinct, cool sensation, right on the upper lip. But as he finished speaking my mind wandered away. Ten days of this? I would go crazy. The pain in my legs was getting unbearable, already one whole leg was reduced to a buzzing mass of pins and needles. At the front of the hall the old students sat like statues, wrapped in shawls. They all looked as if they would be fully enlightened Buddha's before bedtime.

After what seemed like hours Goenka's voice suddenly filled the hall with chanting. It was a strange chant. Very deep with long extension of the vowel sounds. After several minutes chanting he spoke to us again.

'Hmm... Good,' he said smiling, 'take rest now, tomorrow we will start again at four thirty. Remember, observe all the rules and regulations, they are here for your benefit. You have all these people here to serve you, the Dharma policemen,' he chuckled, 'so make the most of this valuable opportunity and remember, of all the rules the most important is silence. The Buddha called the silence of the meditator, 'Noble Silence', so keep Noble Silence and work, no one else can do this for you. You have to work out your own salvation. Try to continue observing the breath at all times, not only when you are sitting in this hall, but while you are walking, eating and resting.'

He smiled like a father to his children,'....hmm, good, now take rest, take rest, take rest.'

It took me several minutes before I could regain the use of my left leg and hobble out of the hall. I was astonished to see some of the old students carry on sitting unmoving. Outside the last of the rich colours of sunset lingered over the moon-scape rocks and bats flitted in and out of the yellow pools of electric light. And silence. The great equaliser. It lay over the camp like magic. The only sounds were footsteps on gravel, a distant train whistle, wailing and lonely, and my thoughts, blathering on, unceasing, the endless stream of internal noise. Me.

For three days we meditated on our breath. According to the teacher we were developing Samadhi, concentration, one pointedness of mind. But I found that as the days went by my mind, rather than becoming quiet, became more and more distracted, my Samadhi consisted of a monologue re-living the past or creating improbable futures. One breath observed to every ten thousand thoughts. Each evening Goenka gave a discourse. For the first time I heard the world explained in a way that fitted in with how I experienced it. This was the Buddha Dharma. According to the Buddha, Goenka taught, all things are constantly changing, there is no object neither mental nor physical in the entire universe that is not in a state of perpetual change.

We were told of the Buddha's four Noble truths. The first was Dukkha, suffering. This was such a relief to hear because, for the most part, my life was suffering. The second noble truth was the cause of suffering, Tanha, desire, hanging onto the pleasant in life and avoiding the unpleasant, in short, craving and aversion. The third truth was Nirodha, the ending of suffering by dealing with the cause, and the fourth was Magga, the path, the way to do it, which, according to our teacher, was to practise the technique of meditation we were learning. I became a convert to Buddhist philosophy without any resistance, but the Vipassana meditation practise was proving more difficult.

On the morning of the fourth day, after three and a half days of unceasing spacing out, Goenka told us that we had one pointed concentration of mind, and with this one pointedness we could move onto the practise of Panna, wisdom. Wisdom! This was what it was all about. I had kept my Sila and completed the three days of Samadhi with my nose and head trips, and now it was time for Wisdom. The ending of suffering, even Nirvana. A big notice board outside the dining hall announced a rearranged schedule for the afternoon. 'Between two and four p.m., Vipassana will be given.' I could hardly wait.

After lunch there was a tangible sense of anticipation in the meditation hall. The sitting began in the usual way with Goenka reminding us to observe our breath. Then, suddenly he changed tack, he asked us to take our attention to the top of our heads and observe whatever sensation we may be feeling. To help out, he ran through a quick menu of possible sensations.

'You may feel a tingling sensation, or an itching sensation. You may feel a throbbing sensation or pulsing sensation. You may feel a sensation like ants crawling. It does not matter what sensation you feel. Just observe that sensation, as it is. It may be pleasant, it may be unpleasant, observe without craving or aversion, with equanimity, remaining alert and attentive.'

I observed the top of my head. It felt, rather disappointingly, like the top of my head. Suddenly my knees began to ache with an unnatural intensity.

Goenka continued, 'From now on we are going to have three

of the one hour sittings each day as Addithan sittings. Addithan means strong determination in Pali. What is our strong determination? It is to remain without moving for the entire hour of meditation, just observing whatever sensation arises.'

Whatever sensation? He had to be kidding. My knees were feeling as if a vice was being closed on them.

Goenka returned us to the sensation at the top of our heads.

'Now move your attention down to the forehead,' he paused, I waited for some new amazing event or instruction, 'observe what ever sensation you feel on your forehead. It may be itching, it may be heat......'

He again listed sensations and asked us to observe them without judging, just seeing their reality as they were, remaining alert and attentive.

We moved on to the sensations in the face. Slowly, and with a sinking feeling, I began to realise that this was it, we were going on a guided tour around the body. The pain in my legs was increasing. As the course was largely for Indians all the instructions were given in both English and Hindi. Forty minutes later we were still on the upper torso.

'....now moving on down to the left lower arm. Feeling what ever sensation there is. It may be....'

I wanted to scream. Who cares about a tickling sensation on the left fore arm when your knees have been dipped in boiling oil and hit with a lump hammer. It was now well past an hour and the process was still several maddening limbs from completion. Finally I could not bear it, and surreptitiously I moved my leg. The pain stopped for a second, then returned with the same intensity to the new position. It was a lost cause. Finally we had almost made it right round the body. I was willing Goenka on through the remaining sections. Come on, upper back, shoulder blades. Come on! Come on! Neck and then, yes! Back of the head and finally the top of the head, feeling what ever sensation..... I stumbled out into the sunlight. So that was Vipassana. Self inflicted torture on a cushion. All I could think was that I wanted my precious sweet tea and piece of fruit.

That evening Goenka's talk explained the Vipassana meditation practice. We spent our lives, he said, running after pleasant sensations, the process of desire, or we tried to avoid unpleasant ones, the process of aversion. This was suffering, endlessly chasing impermanent sensations. This was Samsara, the illusory existence we all inhabit. The antidote was to watch this process and not react, to stop feeding the habit of reaction, using awareness and equanimity as our tools. While all this made perfect sense it was something else all together to sit without moving, and observe all the sensations in the body. I couldn't do it. I could not bear it.

Goenka told us that at first we would experience gross sensations. These gross sensations, which I took to be a euphemism for pain, were habits of the mind locked into the body. By observing sensations and not reacting we would unlock the past, break the old habit of reacting, and begin to purify our minds. Each time we observed a sensation without reacting we untied the patterns associated with that sensation, whether it be anger, or fear, or lust. As time went on we would feel subtler sensations, until we could observe the subtlest arising and passing away, and then maybe we would understand the ultimate truth of arising and passing and be liberated. With the proposition of enlightenment hanging in the air Goenka continued.

'...but this takes a long time so do not be in a hurry. It can take a life time,' he paused, 'or several life times.' He smiled and there was obedient but disappointed laughter.

The days passed very slowly. My mind wandered unceasingly, and I could not stay aware of my sensations whilst moving my attention around my body. If for any prolonged period, like a few minutes, I did manage to practice the technique, the pain in my knees suddenly became unbearable. As the days passed Goenka quickened the movement of our attention until we were told to sweep our attention up and down our bodies, feeling, as he put it, a free flow of subtle sensations. For the dullards he was always adding that the kind of sensation we felt was not important, it was the attention, the non reactive awareness, which was important.

It was no good, by the last few days I had begun to space out as a way to get through the day. I found I could escape the pain by going off into my thoughts, which was nothing new. With the end of the course looming I realised I had no further plans. I had hoped the course would solve everything, but it hadn't. I was still who I was and the problem of being me continued. I still had to do something and I still had no idea what or why, so I began to create my onward journey. A new fantasy. I decided I would hitch hike north. Maybe, I speculated, Eva would travel with me. I saw the two of us, in love, standing by the road, free and happy together. It looked good.

On the tenth day the last period of meditation, before the silence ended, was Metta meditation. Metta is a Pali word meaning loving kindness. The meditation involved filling our hearts and minds with a sense of love and compassion, and then spreading that sense out to take in all beings everywhere. After ten days struggling through our own inner pain this reduced many people to tears. Goenka chanted a lamenting chant and it was all over. Suddenly a free agent again, having to communicate again, I felt afraid and vulnerable. Laurie came up to me.

'Did you have a good course?' he asked kindly.

'I liked the theory,' I said, 'but I don't think the meditation is for me. I think art is more important for me.' It sounded utterly plausible, and as I said it I believed it. So did Laurie. The fear I felt did not show, yet it pervaded the molecules of my body, beyond explanation or definition. Fear was the only real thing, all the rest was fantasy, make believe.

By the time I came to leave I couldn't find Eva, but as soon as I had started talking after the course ended I knew that I would never have the courage to ask her to travel with me. With my bag over my shoulder, I walked alone out of the centre, down through the poverty of Igatpuri and out onto the highway. Crazily decorated, overloaded trucks roared past as I walked along the dusty road side. Once I had cleared the houses I stopped and waited for a lift. After twenty minutes a truck stopped. Two rather unpleasant looking men leered down at me. They obviously hoped I was going to be their entertainment. Feeling far from happy I squeezed into the hot cramped cab and began a noisy, uncomfortable journey north.

I hitch hiked for two days, but it was hard work. Travelling by lorry was slow, uncomfortable and, as I was expected to contribute, worked out more expensive than the train or bus. The drivers who picked me up were not good company, and I spent most of my time either answering inane questions about money and sex, or sitting in an uncomfortable silence. Both evenings I reached depressing, poverty-stricken towns, and in the filthy hotel rooms loneliness engulfed me. Where was I going? Was this what I wanted to be doing with my life? Why was I in India? I re-invented the old long term plan. The plan was like this. After three months in India I would return to England overland, for I had bought a one way ticket, and go to art school. I stuck this threadbare plan over the pain in my mind like a sticking plaster on a wound. Now I felt as if my life was not totally pointless. I was just waiting until I could return to England and go to art school. A sensible thing to do. My life would start from there, finally on a definable course with an ever-increasing sense of meaning and security.

I arrived in Ajmer by train, having given up hitching. From Ajmer I caught a local bus to Pushkar, a fairy tale city built at the edge of a sacred lake. It was a jumble of turrets, lattice windows, domes and arches locking into one another, all reflected in the mirror surface of the lake. Its crowded streets were less romantic. The bazaar was too used to tourists, the prices were high and the service unfriendly. Cows meandered amongst the decaying buildings, and dodgy Brahmin priests did a brisk trade at the lake side ghats, blessing pilgrims after arguing about the cost. The whole place was crumbling, a relic of another time, squatted by the present.

In one of the Pushkar tea shops I met an Australian woman who was leaving Pushkar to go to Mount Abu in south Rajasthan. She told me Mount Abu was a six thousand foot mountain in the flat desert. On its summit there was a temperate green land of lakes and valleys. It had always been a holy mountain, a place of pilgrimage. One evening, as I walked to a tea shop at the end of the village, I was surrounded on the street by three snarling and barking dogs. Reacting in the worst possible way, I made a run for the tea shop entrance. One of the dogs bit me in the leg. An Indian at the chai shop made a paste from chillies and put it on the wound. It was not a bad bite, so I took the chance the dog was not carrying rabies. The alternative of ten injections in the stomach at the local hospital seemed more dangerous. From that moment on I was afraid of the street dogs and they sensed it. They sensed it so strongly they would wake up when I walked past. Pushkar at night became a nightmare, dogs appeared from every corner and attacked me. I started carrying a large stick whenever I went out after dark. I had had enough of Pushkar and, even though it was going back the way I had just come, I caught a night train south again to Mount Abu.

I was woken by the ticket collector in the first light, as the train was slowing. 'Abu Road,' said the ticket collector, as he shook my shoulder.

The train stopped at a small station surrounded by sparse semi desert. Outside was a dusty bus park and a few tea stalls. There was an hour to wait for the first bus up the mountain, so I sat on my bag. My head was pounding and I was beginning to feel very unwell. I started shivering and longed for the sun to rise to warm me. The bus I boarded sat empty for several hours. By the time it departed I was feeling terrible. We set off up the mountain side, winding back and forth. I was getting hot and cold waves and my head hurt, the noisy banging of the bus, and the roar of the engine, which only made rare excursions out of second gear, was torture. After an hour of steep winding roads the bus levelled out into a landscape more like Goa than Rajasthan. Green terraced rice paddies were edged with grass and overflowing irrigation channels; there were palms and tall broad leafed trees, and the air was cool.

I got off the bus only wanting a bed and sleep. I began to climb a long flight of steps built by some town worthy. I looked up and found looking down at me, built by whoever had built the steps, a modern statue of the Buddha with a plaster halo sitting on a plaster lotus, his hands in the teaching position. Beyond the Buddha statue was the Hotel Lake View. It was built on and against the steep rocky hill side, and as the name claimed, it looked out over a small lake.

'You want room? Come on, no problem,' said the manager and took me up steps cut out of the rock. I took the room without even looking at it, all I wanted was to sleep. I collapsed on the iron frame bed with it's lumpy mattress, dragged the rough blankets over me and fell back into sleep oblivion.

For days I lay shivering and sweating as the illness worked

it's way through my body. The tensions and anxieties went with it. I lay, my mind finally silent, breath coming in and breath going out, finally absorbed in the sensations of the present.

After four days I began to venture out, but it was another two before I was eating properly and beginning to get my strength back. I felt more open and relaxed. I felt as if finally I had arrived in India. At a chai shop I met Jean-Paul, a Frenchman. He told me he was living in a deserted hermitage on the hill side behind the large Hindu ashram by the lake. The hermitage had been squatted by a Swami called Swami Om who lived there with his wife. He had picked up Jean-Paul and an Australian girl who were now living there too. So the next day I packed my back pack and followed Jean-Paul, slightly furtively, through the gates of the ashram and out at the back up a winding path.

At the hermitage, a collection of ruined buildings, I met Swami Om, dressed in orange and with long hair and a beard. His wife was an older French woman, she fussed over him like a mother, and looked very worn out. The Australian girl was a loner, she carried her possessions tied in a cloth and went bare foot. Swami Om explained he was a yoga teacher. He was trying to be a Guru but couldn't get it together. He just sat around chatting and smoking joints ending up as stoned and silly as Jean-Paul and me. His wife looked on, anxious and bored, while she washed his clothes and cooked his food. In the cave above us lived a real hermit Yogi. He was as thin as a stick and wore only a loin cloth. He looked very severe and never spoke to us. He was keeper of the sacred spring where we got our drinking water. He spent the day in silent meditation, except in the morning and evening when he came out to do Hatha Yoga and Pujas at the spring side.

The days went by. We celebrated Holi festival by throwing

coloured water over each other, and Swami Om explained the significance of the celebration over a few joints. But the ashram authorities had started to hassle Swami Om. The Australian girl got up one morning and said she was going to walk down the mountain. It was the back of the mountain, away from the road and railway, she planned to walk from village to village. Jean-Paul and I decided it might be better to move on rather than get thrown out. I had been playing my bamboo flute and Swami Om told me about a friend of his who taught Indian music in Dharamsala, a town in the Himalayan foothills. He suggested, when I expressed an interest, that I should go there and learn to play the Indian flute properly. A new plan, another fantasy, took hold in my mind. Rather than continue on a meaningless, sight-seeing trip around India I would go to Dharamsala and study Indian flute. I calculated I could afford to stay about a month before I would be left with only enough money to get home. With my new upgraded plan I set off to Dharamsala and the Himalayas.

Chapter 4

I was woken once again by a ticket collector walking through the train, this time calling, 'Patankot! Patankot!' I wandered down to the end of the carriage, the door was open, and the cool morning air blew in. Below me the endless parched land, sparsely covered in stunted trees, slid past in the grey half light. Holding the door frame I leant out; the sight that greeted me made me cry out in wonder. Ahead in the distance, magnificent and unexpected, bathed in rose pink first light, looking like mountains in a fairy tale, were the snow clad peaks of the Himalayas.

I set off from Patankot bus station aboard a blue and silver Himachel Pradesh Transport Company bus. The plains stopped abruptly and we began to climb into green valleys studded with pine trees. There was water everywhere, and green fields with borders of wild flowers. We passed through bustling country towns, picking up passengers. At each valley the bus became more crowded. The conductor swung up and down between the seats collecting fares. An ancient witch like old woman got on and gave the conductor a fraction of the correct fare; everyone laughed while the conductor remonstrated, knowing she was far beyond the rules of the bus company. A crowd of school girls piled on at the front. They were as pretty as spring flowers, giggling and laughing, exuding innocent sensuality. The conductor weaved his way to them with eel-like skill, but once he reached them, that was far enough. Everyone seemed to be smiling, laughing and chattering as we careered our way around the winding roads. As we reached the small hill towns more and more of the passengers disembarked. Then we began to climb up steeper valleys. At a bend in the road a small boy sat doing his home work, his back to a pine tree. Behind him was an expanse of rolling hills fading into blue.

In Delhi I had learnt that Dharamsala was not only home to Swami Om's friend the music teacher, but was also home to the Dalai Lama, and capital of the Tibetans in exile.

'Don't get off the bus in Dharamsala,' I had been told, 'the last stop is beyond that, up the mountain; it's called McLeod Ganj. That's where the Tibetans live.'

When the bus reached Dharamsala the remaining few passengers and the driver got out. I waited alone in the bus. After a few minutes the driver swung back up into his seat. Leaving Dharamsala behind, the bus wound higher and higher up through the pine forests. We passed an army camp out on a limb of the hill and various tiny roadside hamlets. The pine trees became thick forest, and amongst them I saw a chapel, its moss covered stone walls like some misplaced corner of a Welsh valley. The bus pulled up a final steep incline and came to a halt on a small square of tarmac. It was the end of the road. The driver stood up, opened his door and looked back at me.

'McLeod Ganj,' he said.

McLeod Ganj straddled a narrow ridge. It had two streets, both little more than wide alleyways that were divided by a single row of buildings. They occupied the entire width of the ridge, with the other buildings spilling off the edges, clinging to the hill side. Between these buildings all I could see was hazy blue sky, dotted with buzzards circling in the updraughts.

I stood by the bus with my bag, but no one paid me any attention. The Tibetan people looked out from their shops, others, less wealthy, squatted by the road side selling cheap clothes. A young, pretty Tibetan woman, holding hands with a small boy, walked past and smiled at me. It was an open friendly smile, a smile to welcome a visitor. Unlike in the towns

of the plains below no one hassled me, which was almost dis-
concerting. I took a room at the Green Hotel. I stood on its
balcony, looked out over the Himalayan foothills and felt an
enormous sense of relief. After years travelling, moving from
place to place, never at peace with myself, I felt that I had
finally arrived. I felt as if I had come home.

I spent the next few days taking walks around the village.
The March weather was cool and there were puddles on the
roads. I longed for my jeans and shoes, which I had posted off
to Calcutta when in Goa, but had to flop along in socks, flip
flops and cotton pyjamas. One evening I fell into conversation
with two Austrians who turned out to be students of music
with Swami Om's friend at the Minu Cottage music school in
Dharamsala. The next morning I followed them down the
mountain in glorious sunshine. The winding path was surrounded by rhododendrons full of spring blooms. After twenty
minutes we came out onto a narrow metalled road, which led
us past a large complex of Tibetan looking buildings. My
friends told me it was the Tibetan Library. The Tibetans were
not inhibited by hills when it came to building.

Below the Tibetan library was Minu Cottage. Minu Cottage
was not particularly cottage like. It was a two story concrete
building, on a triangle of land sandwiched within a sharp bend
of the road. This road was the back road to McLeod from
Dharamsala. It was a very steep climb and little used, except
by jeeps and the occasional Indian lorry shredding its clutch
plates in a desperate attempt to deliver building materials to
the ever-expanding Tibetans.

On the Minu Cottage concrete veranda sat Swami Om's
friend with a couple of westerners in a haze of hashish smoke.
His name was, rather vaguely, just Swami-ji. He was very like
Swami Om, with even longer hair, and he was dressed in the
same orange robes. I thought he looked equally unconvincing

as a holy man. He was just an orange hippie. Like Om, he liked smoking hash and insisted I smoke with him. After the chillum I explained how I wished to study Indian flute, and that Swami Om had recommended him as a teacher. Would he, I asked humbly, be able to take me on as a pupil?

'No problem,' said Swami-ji.

At the end of the scrubby garden, beside the road, was a makeshift tea shop. A sign outside declared, 'Ashoka's Tea shop.' Ashoka was the manager of Minu Cottage, so I asked him if there were any rooms free. The cost of living at the Green hotel and eating all my meals in restaurants was relatively high, I wanted to buy a stove and cook my own food, I wanted to stop being a tourist. Ashoka said there was a small room free with a larger room becoming available soon.

The first week at Minu cottage I was busy setting up home, making trips to the bazaar in Dharamsala, buying all the bits and pieces for cooking. I enjoyed the sense of living in a place rather than just passing through. After a week, just as Ashoka had said, another room became free. It was a fine room with a big window giving me an unobstructed view along the eastern edge of the Himalayas.

Downstairs on the veranda lived a collection of stoned musicians. They got up late, stayed up late and were surrounded by sitars, guitars and tablas. They always seemed to be in the process of loading, lighting or smoking chillums. They were friendly and always offered me a smoke if I was passing. I quickly learnt not to take them up on this after spending several days coping with the effects. Once stoned I would walk the mountain paths my mind exploding, every thought seeming like a momentous insight while the world was unwrapped, shimmering with intensity and beauty. But it was exhausting, and I would return drained, my head hurting needing to sleep. The musicians would still be there, relaxed, jamming along, still smoking. I wondered how they managed it.

I started to take flute lessons with Swami-ji. I had never seriously studied the flute before, I had just played for my own pleasure. At first it was interesting, learning Indian scales and simple rhythms, but as time went on it began to become tedious. I had not considered what it would mean to study Indian music. It had been part of a fantasy about doing something useful with my time in India, a way of dealing with the discontent I felt. As it was, just looking after myself was quite time consuming. It involved shopping expeditions to Dharamsala on a daily basis, cooking needed preparation time and washing up at the pump. In between, along with my reducing flute practice, I painted water colours, read, or went for walks in the warm spring sunshine and, occasionally, I tried to meditate.

After a few weeks Swami-ji moved on. His place was taken by a serious young man who did not smoke hash, and was completely committed to classical Indian music. I had a few lessons with him, but it was painfully obvious I did not have the discipline, desire or talent. Finally, embarrassed, I spoke to the new teacher. He smiled when I told him I was stopping the lessons; it was a relief for both of us. A few days later I met him walking alone along a narrow footpath on the mountain side. I was carrying some wild flowers which I intended to paint. He stopped and admired them, telling me their names in Hindi.

'I'm going to paint them,' I told him.

He smiled, and said generously, 'you have your own wisdom.'

In the houses around Minu Cottage lived various westerners who were studying Tibetan Buddhism at the library. In one house lived an English woman studying Tibetan art. I was interested by this connection between art and Buddhism. As I seemed unable to practice the teachings of the Buddha through meditation, I thought perhaps I could practice them through drawing. It could be a way to connect myself with the Buddha Dharma, to sit drawing Buddhas instead of sitting in meditation. I asked her if she thought her teacher would accept me as a pupil. She explained how I should approach him, taking gifts of fruit, tea and the traditional Kata, a white scarf of greeting.

A few days later, armed with my gifts and a collection of my drawings, I arrived at Champla's house, which was close by Minu Cottage. Champla was an aristocrat, one of the most skilled Tibetan artists in exile, and the Dalai Lama's official artist. I found him sitting outside his house, painting on the earth veranda. He was wearing traditional Tibetan clothes, and had rows of silver rings in his ears. Champla wore his hair in two long plaits, interwoven with red cord and turquoise beads and wrapped around his head. He looked just like the American Indians in old photos, all he needed was a Winchester in his lap. When he saw me he smiled, beckoned me to come near, and called for his daughter. She came out of the house. She was twelve or thirteen and very composed; she acted as translator. Champla looked through my drawings. He seemed highly amused by my work, turning the pages chuckling, as if looking through humorous cartoons. I was told to return in a few days and I would be given my first grid of an unrobed Buddha.

The Buddha grid was calculated according to strict rules, and the Buddha image had to fit exactly to the proportions it defined. As a pupil I would have to copy these grids until I could reproduce them to the satisfaction of the teacher. It was the traditional form of teaching, developed in Tibet for students who had probably never drawn anything before they began their training. For me as a western art student to reproduce these simple line drawings was a relatively easy task, but

I took it all very seriously. I wanted to believe the image was imbibed with a sacred perfection that transcended mere egotistical draughtsmanship, so when Champla gave me my first grid of an unrobed Buddha I felt as if I were embarking on an esoteric journey. I threw myself into the task of recreating the image in every detail. I hoped the perfection of the form would leak out into my mind.

The weeks passed by, the days became hotter and summer came to the mountains. My days were now spent earnestly drawing Buddhas. Occasionally I still tried to meditate. This had a strange effect on my physiology, for as soon as I sat in the cross-legged posture and paid attention to my breath and sensations, I became unbearably agitated. The agitation came in waves, wriggling down my nerves like a forerunner to a fit. It made my heart beat so hard it frightened me. So I didn't meditate too much, instead I sat cross legged and painted Buddhas. Then I had no problem, I could sit for hours.

One day, as I sat gazing out of my window, I saw something else that made my heart start beating hard. Walking down the road from McLeod Ganj was Eva. I rushed out to greet her, embarrassed by my racing heart and uneven voice. We went together to Ashoka's chai shop for tea. We exchanged the details of where we had been since the meditation course. Eva was meditating every day.

'Where are you staying?' I asked her.

'Oh,' she said vaguely, 'I have a place in the forest. It is very quiet, good for meditation.'

A place in the forest! It sounded wonderful. I suddenly felt embarrassed by Minu Cottage.

'Minu Cottage is fairly quiet,' I said, 'until a passing truck gets stuck on the bend.'

Eva laughed and her laughter seemed to promise the ending of all suffering.

'Are you going to the bazaar in Dharamsala?' I asked.

'Well, no,' she said, 'I am going to see a Tibetan artist. I am learning with him.'

'Not Champla! But that's such a coincidence,' I cried, delighted that our lives were now inescapably joined, 'I'm also studying with him.'

'Oh,' said Eva.

Eva was unfathomable; one moment I would feel as if her heart was about to be mine for ever, the next she was virtually a stranger. We talked for a while, but then abruptly she got up.

'I must go now,' she said.

'Look,' I said, 'do drop in and see me when you pass.'

She gave me a look and a smile of such warmth that I was already speculating about our next meeting before she had turned the corner.

From that day forward I lived for the moment when Eva would appear around the bend in the road. She came to see Champla every two or three days, usually during the late morning. I tried not to wait, and I pretended to be doing other things, but I could not concentrate on anything else in case I missed her. Sometimes she would come in for tea, but other days, keeping her gaze determinedly straight ahead, she would walk on past. A few weeks later I was in for another shock. As I walked up the road to McLeod, Eva came around a bend and by her side, chatting away animatedly, was Laurie. My blood ran cold. I could not believe it. He was here too.

'Hello Ken !' cried Laurie warmly and Eva gave me one of her most sexy smiles yet.

'Hello Laurie,' I said, as if meeting him was only of minimal passing interest, 'are you staying around here?'

'Yes,' Laurie told me, 'I'm living up in the forest near Eva.'

Eva smiled at us both warmly.

I clung to my daily Buddha drawing sessions. I had now progressed onto the robed Buddha. Using one of my best draw-ings, which I had water coloured, I made an altar. I framed the picture and placed it on a shelf with a Tibetan white scarf over it, and in front, in a small brass pot, I put wild flowers. I had never had an altar before, it was strangely comforting.

By now I had enough money left to get me back overland if I travelled fast and lived cheap, but I could not bring myself to leave. I began to put back my departure date. Finally I decided I would stay for the summer in Dharamsala, then borrow enough from my parents to return in the autumn. I decided to look for another place to stay. The hash smoking music scene of Minu Cottage was not the environment I wanted for draw-ing Buddhas. I began looking around but I could not find any-thing I liked. Then one morning Eva made a rare appearance at my door.

'Are you still looking for another room?' she asked, 'there is a room coming free at Balcony house where I live.'

I could not believe my ears. To live in the same house as Eva. To see her every day. It seemed too good to be true.

Eva went on, 'If you like to come up and see the room this afternoon you could stay for supper....'

An evening invitation, a romantic dinner for two. It could only mean one thing, and as the door closed behind her I was already convinced we were at last to be lovers.

I set out during the late afternoon and walked up the road from Minu Cottage to McLeod Ganj. Once in the village I fol-lowed the map Eva had given me. At the far end of the McLeod Ganj bazaar I found the steep jeep track she had drawn on her map. It zigzagged up the hillside, crowded in by the village houses. After a few hundred feet the refugee village stopped and there was only forest. I walked slowly, the track was as steep as a staircase. After twenty minutes, near the top of the hill, I found myself looking down onto a small meadow.

On one side was a long squat two-story building set back against the hill. The walls were rough stone and mud, and the wide roof was covered in uneven, corrugated iron. In front of the two upstairs rooms there was a long crude balcony, and beneath it in front of the downstairs rooms was an earth veranda. Eva sat on a charpoy on the veranda, painting. On the far side of the meadow the ground fell sharply away. Wind gently rustled through the tree tops and crows called into the silence; the view was of emptiness. Minu Cottage and Dharamsala suddenly seemed like an urban sprawl. I walked over to Eva and, as I was still breathless from the walk, sat for a while on the edge of the veranda getting my breath back.

'What a beautiful place,' I said finally.

Eva looked first at me, then out between the pines.

'Yes, it is beautiful,' she agreed, and continued painting.

The wind caressed the trees like distant waves.

'A fine place to work,' I said.

Eva considered this remark for an uncomfortably long time.

'Yes,' she agreed finally, 'I like painting here.'

I sat staring hopelessly out into the emptiness.

'Later,' said Eva, after a long silence, 'we can walk over and visit Laurie, perhaps he would like to come and eat with us too.'

'Yes,' I said, 'perhaps he would.'

I had a wait of two weeks before I could move to Balcony house, and I decided to spend some of the time at Triund. Triund was the last ridge before the snow-capped, Dahuladar mountain peaks up behind McLeod. I had been told there was an old colonial bungalow where I would be able to stay. I was tired of Minu cottage, I was tired of waiting to see if Eva would show up and I wanted a complete break. So I packed my back pack with provisions and walked up the road to McLeod, then on up, past Balcony house, and onto an old but well made path through rhododendron forests. The path wound steeply up the side of the valley, and each time I stopped to rest the view behind me became more spectacular and the path ahead steeper. When I finally reached the top, after a six hour climb, I was on meadow of cropped grass as smooth as a golf course. In the distance I could hear the familiar sound of sheep. Behind me the view was so wide I felt I could see the curve of the planet. The far side of the meadow dropped steeply down into a densely wooded valley. On the far side of this valley, climbing out of the trees, was one great, six-thousand-foot wall of unbroken rock. There was snow at its distant top. Looking up from McLeod only the top part of the mountain showed above the Triund ridge, like an ice berg tip above the surface of the ocean. Now I stood staring, trying to adjust my mind to take in its enormity, I felt I should fall to my knees and bow down.

At the far end of the meadow was the colonial bungalow. It looked absurd, like a toy, a misplaced bit of an Edwardian railway station. When I walked closer I could see it was bare and decayed. I pushed open the stiff door. In the tiled suburban fire place there were blackened rocks, set to support a saucepan. A heap of firewood lay near by, dead branches dragged in from the forest, scattered around on the old floor boards. Eva was sitting drawing at a long table.

'Hello Eva,' I said.

'Hello,' she replied with a smile so vulnerable I longed to hug her, 'so you have come here too.'

The way she said it, it could have meant anything.

There were seven other travellers staying at the bungalow, all of different nationalities. Over the following days we became a community, sharing our food and, in the evenings, sharing our thoughts with an intimacy I had only experienced before with my closest friends. I felt we were graced by the mountains, their silence and beauty filling us with a quietness of heart and mind. Often in the early morning I would walk barefoot down the steep path on the far side of the meadow to collect water. It was a long walk down through the lichen covered oaks to the valley bottom. There, a stream ran from under the edge of compacted snow. Carrying a bucket of icy water I would return up the path absorbed into the vast silence. Sometimes I would see Eva, sitting alone, perfectly still, meditating between the trees in a pool of early sunshine, the light catching her hair.

One day at the house, standing behind her as she drew at the table, I caressed her hair just once, almost as though I were caressing the head of a child. She got up abruptly and, without a word, walked out. She did not return until many hours later.

'I thought you had left us,' I half joked on her return.

'So did I,' she replied with a shy smile.

None of us wanted to go back down the mountain, but as the days passed our food was running out. Finally we were left with only one meal of rice, onions and black tea.

The next morning people began to set off. I walked back with Eva. She was in good spirits, and we laughed and talked as we walked easily downhill through the morning light, but as we neared the bottom of the trail Eva began to hang back. She stopped talking and would not look at me. In the end I gave up and walked ahead angrily without saying good-bye.

The room at Balcony house was far rougher than my old room at Minu Cottage. The walls were covered in mud, cracked crazily all over like a dried-up water hole. Rush mats had been tied between the roof beams and the space above stuffed with newspaper for insulation. As the rooms in Balcony house went it was well equipped. There was a wonky table for storing food and cooking, a crude wooden bed with uneven planks, but no mattress, and a wicker table and chair. But I did not really care much about the room because it was merely an appendage to the balcony. The balcony was wonderful. It looked out through the trees and, above all, it was light. I had the end section, which I set up as an outdoor room. I returned to the room only to sleep. I would have slept on the balcony too, but I was fearful of spiders and scorpions.

I settled back into daily sessions of iconography, but the feeling I was achieving very little artistically was beginning to nag at the back of my mind. My basic aim was still to spend some time each day sitting still and keeping the Buddha in my life. I developed a routine; I would work for two or three days and complete three or four Buddha images, then make the trip to lower Dharamsala to see Champla, where I would have the drawings 'corrected'. Champla seemed to accept my endless visits with equanimity. Each time I arrived he would check my drawings, make some nominal changes in red pencil like a primary school teacher, smile, nod and send me off to draw some more. It was a big day for me when he gave me a new deity to start on, as it meant I had drawn the previous one to his satisfaction. To my eye there was little difference between the drawings I brought, but I surrendered to his authority; he was the master. I had completed a robed Sakyamuni Buddha, a Green Tara the goddess of compassion, and was now working on Vajrapani, a wrathful deity, protector of the Dharma. Occasionally I noticed a look of irritation on Champla's face when I proudly arrived with yet another handful of identical drawings. I did not like to think too closely about why Champla might find my arrival irritating. It was the first time for many years my life had any structure, and I was enjoying it. I felt that at last I was achieving something.

At Balcony house I had one main distraction, Eva. I could see her through gaps in the balcony floor boards. When I first moved in Eva had ignored me with icy determination. But I did not push myself on her, and she softened a little over the weeks. But our friendship was much cooler now than it had been when I lived at Minu Cottage. Yet the whole time I was painfully aware of her existence below me. If she went out I would wait, unable to forget, listening hour after hour for the sound of the chain on her door on her return. Equally, as the stone steps up to the balcony were by her room, when I went out or returned I had to pass by her charpoy. Would she be there? Would she look up? Would she greet me or ignore me? I tried to coincide my visits to Champla with Eva's. She would agree to walk down the mountain with me, but she always made sure we visited him separately. Occasionally on the way back we met in McLeod, in one of the Tibetan restaurants. At these rendezvous she would unexpectedly let her guard down, charm me with her laughter and smiles, and give me tender looks that filled me with hope and fuelled my longing.

The room next to mine at Balcony house was occupied by a small, thin, very worried looking woman called Lucy. She was a very devoted but fairly mad Tibetan Buddhist who had been in India for five years. She had had a vision on her way to Delhi airport when about to return to Australia after her first six months in India. From the airport bus she had seen a Tibetan Lama standing in a rice field surrounded by golden light, signalling to her. She understood from his signals that she should stay in India and devote herself to Tibetan Buddhism. Lucy looked in great pain and smoked incessantly, her cigarettes held awkwardly in tense straight fingers. She was tentative and spoke with a tiny whispering voice. Once or twice I witnessed her get angry, and was amazed at her transformation. She metamorphasized from a mouse into a monster. Her voice dropped several octaves and a stream of violent and improbable accusations were hurled at the person who had been foolish enough to cross her.

As we were close neighbours, I always made a point of being

especially polite and friendly in my dealings with Lucy, and she never got angry with me. I was not particularly threatening and I did my best to stick to uncontentious topics of conversation. At times this was difficult, as she would come out with the most extraordinary things.

'Did you know that the Dalai Lama is in telepathic communication with the American Indian chiefs?' she whispered down the balcony to me one day over breakfast.

'Is he?' I replied carefully, 'I wasn't aware of that.'

'No,' she whispered, 'not many people are.'

On another occasion she asked me if I had noticed any thing odd in my room.

'Odd?' I asked uneasily, 'how odd do you mean?'

'Well,' whispered Lucy, 'my room is possessed by powerful forces of evil, they seem to be in the corner by the connecting door to your room. I wondered if you had seen anything on your side.'

'I haven't but I'll keep an eye out tonight,' I told her. And I did, peeping over my bed clothes.

In the room below mine, next door to Eva, lived Claire. She was also pretty crazy, but in a gentle way, not in the same league as Lucy. Claire was tall and had long dark hair. She always wore the same long, rather shapeless dress the colour of earth. She sat in the depths of her dark room reading by the light of a single bulb. Claire was lost deep in her mind. She had become totally passive and so spaced out that talking with her was like talking to someone very far away in a large hall. She seemed to have no emotions, as if in perpetual shock.

Next door to Claire, in rooms built onto the side of Balcony house, lived Jack. Jack had a very large dog, called Rebel. Most of the local dogs were a skinny ingratiating lot which, if you threw them a paltry scrap and gave them a pat, would become instant friends greeting you with wild tail wagging.

Rebel was not like this at all. Jack had nurtured him on meat and bones from the McLeod Ganj butchers, and Rebel had grown muscled, with a taste for flesh, rather than old chapatis. Alongside being muscled, Rebel was also racist. Unlike the other bazaar dogs which were on the receiving end of punishment, Rebel was the one handing it out. Passing Indians and Tibetan monks were regularly pinned to a tree while Rebel raged at their feet. Jack would call Rebel off, but with a casual air that gave the impression he did not quite believe the monk, shepherd or whoever, was entirely the innocent party.

Jack had been in McLeod for many years. He did not talk much with the other short stay Balcony house residents. We were mere six-month tourists, a lowly cast in the caste system of travellers. We were in fact only fractionally better than the three month tourists, those who passed through the hotels of McLeod Ganj clutching guide books, hurrying through India having an experience, before returning home to take up safe careers. They were the untouchables.

Jack was very keen on astrology. He had worked out that the world order as we knew it would end in nineteen eighty-four. This was a popular belief in McLeod Ganj among people who predicted such things. With the cold war at its height this theory did not seem that far-fetched. Astrologers would go into great detail about the various oppositions and conjunctions of planets during nineteen eighty-four that meant some kind of apocalyptic change was inevitable. There were long and complicated extrapolations of how the collapse would happen. The western banking system would fall, or the Soviet Union would invade western Europe. The beginning of a new age, and the destruction of the old. It was assumed that McLeod Ganj, high above the world, would be the home of the untouched few.

Each year Jack went to Kerala and bought a year's supply of Kerala ganja which he brought back to the mountains in a tin trunk. Jack smoked a lot of this ganja. He rolled up joints four inches long and half-an-inch thick which he smoked alone. He always seemed to be rolling up or smoking one when I passed by. I knew about Kerala ganja, it was strong stuff, a joint the size of a cotton bud was enough to start me hallucinating. Another of Jack's peculiarities was that he stammered, but when Jack sang Bob Dylan songs at the top of his voice, amazingly he did not stammer at all. So every one knew when Jack was at home because the forest was filled with his renditions of the songs of Bob Dylan.

One day Lucy whispered to me, as if apologising, that she was going. She planned to attend some teachings being given by a Lama in Nepal. Sally moved into her room. Sally was a Goenka student who had been on the same meditation course with me in January. She was easy-going after Lucy. We began shopping for each other and cooking together. We hung out on the balcony during the warm evenings, chatting by candle-light. Sally had left her job as a social worker in Hackney and also her radical feminist friends, she was seriously seeking the cause of suffering. She read a lot of Dharma books and she planned to sit more meditation courses.

The next time I visited Champla he looked at my most recent drawings and did no corrections. This usually meant he considered I had reproduced a good likeness, and I would be given another deity to start work on. I was chalking them up. This particular day he was busy and did not give me another grid. I returned hopefully a few hours later. Champla still did not have a new drawing ready, and was visibly annoyed by my reappearance. He got up crossly and went into his house, returning a few moments later with a drawing. He gave it to me brusquely, and then sat down and carried on working. I walked out confused and embarrassed. As I began the walk back up to McLeod, I looked at the drawing he had given me.

It was clearly not one of his own, but had been drawn by a student. As I looked at it I realised it was not a very good drawing at all. It was not the perfect form. I was completely thrown into a quandary, how could I copy a bad drawing? I felt as if I had had the carpet pulled from under my feet. The order and discipline I had created were shattered. I looked at the picture again; the drawing was of Manjushri, the Tibetan deity of wisdom.

Chapter 5

It was high summer, the days were hot and the nights were warm. With the routine of going up and down to Champla ended, my life became much quieter. I began painting home made Thankas, and the only time I left the hill top was to go to Mcleod to get provisions. As there was no running water at Balcony house each day I had to walk with a bucket to a spring on the far side of the hill. I loved this walk along a narrow footpath winding between the pines. I settled into living in the forest, feeling at peace surrounded by its beauty and I was beginning to wonder how I would ever leave. Out of the blue Eva announced her visa had almost expired and she was going to Dalhousie to try to get an extension as she had heard it was easy there. A few days later, very early in the morning, I heard the familiar sound of Eva's door chain and then she was gone.

I drew my pictures, Sally sat at her end of the balcony reading the teachings of various great masters, downstairs Claire lived in the gloom and Jack sang. The sun shone and all was peaceful. But there was a change in the air. It was June, in a few weeks the Monsoon would begin, and this became a frequent topic of conversation. Sometimes there would be just an odd day of rain, but at other times it would be endless cloud that enveloped everything. I heard about the terrible damp, how matches would have to be kept next to the skin wrapped in plastic, how clothes would never dry if washed, how mushrooms grew out of your shoes and how the grass was full of leeches.

Laurie had been living that summer at Glenmore, an old colonial house twenty minutes walk from Balcony house. Glenmore house was owned by a wealthy Indian who occasionally visited in the summer. The out buildings of Glenmore, where the servants would have lived, were now where the travellers lived. The biggest of the out-buildings was a long house of five rooms fronted by a wide veranda. People were always hanging out on this veranda, with a joint or chillum on the go. The middle room was lived in by a very long time resident of McLeod Ganj called Joan. Joan had been many years in India, and although she was always broke somehow she had always managed to make ends meet. Joan had a special quality; the shift of consciousness that came with making India home. She was no longer a tourist, or even a traveller, and it was clear she was not going back. Joan was the undisputed queen of Glenmore. She practised astrology, tantric arts, occultism and some sort of esoteric Buddhism which she washed down with vast amounts of hashish. I was rather in awe of her. In the caste system of westerners, Joan was definitely a Brahmin.

Glenmore was a place where I could turn up unannounced, get stoned and hang out. When I wanted to leave I could get up and go. There was no need for formalities. It was a place where you were not invited to stay, but not expected to go. There were always unusual people arriving to stay. There was Jessica, in her late forties, who had been a prison psychiatrist, and had arrived in India after being declared clinically insane. After several months she had ended up destitute in an isolated village temple in a prohibited area of south India. The villagers, treating her as a Devi, a goddess, had brought her food, so she had stayed there until soldiers found her five months later. An Englishman called Stacy arrived, a Tibetan Buddhist who lived in a remote valley in Zanskar. He spent the winters in retreat in a cave at sixteen thousand feet, cut off from the world for three months. After all the posturing and crankiness of McLeod he was a truly impressive character. Stacy had a quality of attention in his interactions, but he was not trying to impress, nor trying to be cool in the way so many were. He was not cool, but warm. He was alert and present, listening with equal attention to whoever spoke. At one time an old Tibetan Lama, one of his teachers, came to visit Glenmore. While everyone else sat around in tongue-tied awe, Stacy sat holding his hand, chatting and joking with him in Tibetan. Laurie told me it was hard to be sure when Stacy left as he had no luggage. He would just stroll off to the bazaar and not return.

Laurie and I were fast becoming friends. We shared the same enquiry, talking together for hours about the goings-on of the mind. We discussed meditation and the Dharma, we talked about being on the road. Finally, during a walk around the main Temple and Dalai Lama's residence, on a footpath that wound around the hill littered with prayer flags and prayer stones, I broached the subject of Eva.

'You know I like Eva a lot,' I said.

'Yes,' he said smiling, 'that was pretty obvious.'

'Well', I continued, 'sometimes we got on really well and I thought she liked me, but then it was as if shutters came down and she completely cut me out. She would give me loads of come-on's one moment but then, when I tried to get close, she would cut me out. It was pretty confusing.'

'She did that with me too,' said Laurie, 'one minute blowing hot and the next, ice cold.'

I looked at him and smiled in relief, 'so it isn't just me!' I said.

'Of course it's not you,' said Laurie and we both laughed.

We had both tried to court her, and it created a bond between us as we sat there amongst the fluttering prayer flags.

Eva came back from Dalhousie. She had been unable to get a visa extension and was returning to Sweden. She only stayed one night at Balcony House, then she left again for Delhi to sort out her flight. When she came back from Delhi she moved down to the Green Hotel. A few days later her boy friend arrived. I knew they had flown to India together, but they had travelled separately. It seemed typical for Eva to have a boyfriend she never saw. Having been separated from him for six months, she chose his arrival as the moment to visit me at Balcony House. She arrived full of smiles and sexuality. She sat with me on the balcony, something she had never done while she lived there, and was utterly charming. She stayed for hours and talked more intimately than she ever had before. Eva was not happy about leaving McLeod and returning to Sweden, and to make things worse, the night before she left, she got dysentery. I saw her off at the bus stand, looking pale, sad and withdrawn. A thousand miles by public transport to Bombay, I thought the journey would kill her, but a few weeks later I got a post card from Sweden. She wrote, 'Life here is very difficult....'

A few days after Eva went, Laurie left for Hunza in north Pakistan. Claire moved to a more monsoon resistant house higher up the hill. Everyone seemed to be leaving. The village was quiet with most of the hotels empty. Up at Balcony house there was now only me, Sally and Jack downstairs. The empty rooms left Balcony house quiet, as if waiting for something or somebody. Jack's singing became almost reassuring.

The first wave of the monsoon finally arrived. This was not the monsoon proper, but a fore runner, the fringes. Sally and I sat on the balcony and watched the white clouds come creeping across the plains towards us, covering the land like a white tide. The clouds swallowed lower Dharamsala, then came up the mountain side and enveloped McLeod. Finally the mist began to snake through the trees in front of Balcony house, it became thicker and was finally upon us. We were enveloped in a cold, damp, misty silence. That night it began to rain, strong hard rain, and it rained all night. Water cascaded off the tin roof. Buckets and saucepans littered my floor, catching drips from the numerous leaks. It rained all the next day and all the next night. By this time the water running off the roof was clean, giving us an abundance of fresh water. Washing-up became easy. I would line the pans and plates under the streamlets that ran off the corrugated iron roof, and collect them completely clean a few hours later.

After two days and two nights of continual rain, the clouds suddenly vanished and the sun shone again. I grasped the moment and set off to the Bazaar to see Mrs Nowrowji. Mrs Nowrowji was my landlady. She was a Parsi, an ancient descendant of what had once been a great trading family that had owned much of the land around McLeod Ganj. She kept a decaying, empty and incredibly dusty shop in the village. It was trapped in a nineteen thirties time warp, with the shelves and cabinets lined with pre-war newspapers, and stocked with dusty ancient packets that looked as if they had been there for decades.

'Mrs Nowrowji,' I began, 'my roof is leaking and I won-dered.....'

'You see,' interrupted Mrs Nowrowji, ' you people never pay your rent.'

'But I have always paid my....'

Mrs Nowrowji was not interested; she gestured for me to be quiet.

'.... and you are always leaving and not informing me. Informing me of your departure is your duty as tenants. Isn't it?' she did not want an answer, 'You people take rooms, and sub-let them to others, and share rooms which are only single rooms. Yes, I know you people are doing these things. It makes things very difficult for me. Also you people do not wash properly.'

I wanted to point out that the property she let had no running water, no toilets, no bathroom and was a rat and flea infested heap, but kept to the matter in hand.

'Well I'm sorry about all that, but actually at the moment the roof is leaking and I wondered if you had any pitch?'

Mrs Nowrowji surveyed me mistrustfully.

'The chowkidar has some pitch, I will send him round tomorrow.'

To my surprise, a few days later the chowkidar turned up with an ancient blackened pot of rock hard pitch. I built a fire, heated up the pitch, then carrying the pot I climbed precariously onto the tin roof. I was concerned that I would not be able to identify which were the nail holes that leaked, so I had Sally in my room ready to tap the roof in the right spot. I need not have worried. Instead of nail heads, the roof was dotted with small volcanoes of pitch which had obviously been built up over many monsoons. I added my offering to the existing blobs and climbed back down.

All that was left was to wait for the next rains. We did not have to wait long. The next day the clouds came back and the rain began again. I hung some clothes under the balcony roof to dry. Days later they were as wet as when I'd hung them out. When I drew, the paper began to tear under my pencil point, and the pages of Sally's books began to curl. She decided it was time to go. We talked over together her various options. In the end she decided to go to Sri Lanka to a Buddhist retreat centre. I saw her off at the bus stand on what was becoming a rare sunny morning. I was now alone at Balcony house, apart from Jack. I was vaguely aware of his comings and goings, occasionally hearing his door bang shut. The clouds came and enveloped the house in a silence that seemed to suck all sound into it. Even Jack was humbled by it, and he stopped singing.

After another week of rain the sun broke through the clouds. Invigorated by the sunshine I took a bucket bath on the meadow with cold rain water. Then to shake off the claustro-phobic feeling of the mist I set off for a long walk through the sun filled forest. I arrived back in McCleod at mid day and went for a chai. As I drank my tea the clouds returned and it began to rain. I had started to feel ill, shivering in my thin shirt, so I went to a hotel and asked if I could sleep in one of their rooms for a few hours. I lay down shivering uncontrollably. I put every blanket in the room over me until the coldness finally ebbed away and I slipped into sleep. I awoke later in the after-noon, the rain had stopped and I walked back to Balcony house. I found the climb hard and arrived on the meadow feel-ing very ill. The clouds had come back, and in the swirling grey mist the house looked desolate. In my room I fell again into a deep sleep. When I awoke it was dark. Realising I had not eaten since breakfast, I got out of bed, sat on my door step and cooked some scrambled eggs, but when I tried to eat I felt sick. I threw the eggs over the edge of the balcony. I made some tea but found I couldn't drink it. I went back to bed and fell asleep as the rain began to clatter on the tin roof.

The 'Dhood wallah', the milk man, an Indian villager who sold his surplus milk, woke me the next morning rattling my door. I opened the door and needing a pee, I tried to walk down the balcony, but the world closed in on me and the veranda seemed to tip up at an odd angle. I collapsed in a heap against the wall at the top of the stairs. The Dhood wallah watched perplexed.

After a minute or so my head cleared. With a great effort I half walked, half crawled back and sat down on my door step.

'I'm sick,' I told him. I found an empty saucepan for the milk. The dhood wallah was looking very concerned.

'You go to Doctor,' he said.

'Yes, yes. I'll be OK. Thanks,' I added, giving him a weak smile.

After he left I sat for a while on the door step. The mist

swirled along the balcony and chilled me. I tried to get back to the bed, but I had to support myself then launch off in the direction I wanted, trying to reach my goal before the blackness floored me. Back in the bed I found that once I lay down the dizziness went away. The trouble was I still needed an urgent pee. I got out of bed and took a few steps towards the far side of the room. I got about four feet before my legs gave way. I squatted on the floor, laying my head on my knees, then I took another few steps. In this way I negotiated the length of the room. I returned with an empty plastic Jerry can. Sitting down I peed into the plastic container, and then pushed it underneath the bed. Suddenly I craved hot sweet lemon juice. I made the long journey to the balcony and managed to make hot lemon on my stove. The warm sweet lemon was like nectar and I drank it sitting in the door way. Leaving everything littered around on the balcony I went back to bed and almost instantly slept again.

When I next awoke the day had passed and it was dark. I sat unsteadily on the edge of my bed, peed into the Jerry can then pushed it back out of sight. Once again I craved hot lemon, but I dreaded the process of making it. Slowly I reached my door and sat on the step. Outside was a black misty silence. I made another glass of hot lemon, then returned to my bed, happy to be able to close the door behind me. It began to rain heavily, and the rain on the tin roof filled the room with a dull roar. I lay looking up at the sagging rush mats tied between the roof beams. They bulged and sagged down the room like the belly of a huge lizard. A rat scuttled across one of the mats disturbing the screwed up newspaper. A fine spray of gritty dust rattled onto the floor below. I turned out the light. The rain hissed on. Somewhere in the darkness a drip began a steady pat-pat-pat on the floor.

I was awoken the next morning by the Dhood wallah's two

young boys.

'No milk! I don't want milk,' I cried weakly from my bed.

They continued to rattle the door. I staggered over to the door, opened it and slumped on the step. The milk from the day before lay curdled in the pan. I threw it over the edge of the balcony and, without bothering to wash it, poured the new milk in. The two boys watched unmoved.

'No more milk,' I told them, 'milk finish!'

They wouldn't go.

'Give me cigarette,' demanded the eldest.

'No, no, go away,' I begged. They watched me, hesitating, unsure of how far to push.

'Go on, go!' I cried desperately, 'Finish, Go.... Chello!' and they left me.

A thick, cold mist hung in the silent air. Only the dull trunks of the trees punctuated the white gloom. I made hot lemon and retreated into the safety of my room. Back in bed I lay down painfully on the cotton filled mattress. I could feel the irregular planks beneath. I felt tired. Nothing more. No thoughts, no questions, just tiredness. I fell asleep again.

I woke in the middle of the night with the room filled with intense white light. A second later the whole house shook under a massive clap of thunder, and the rain increased in intensity. I lay listening, waiting, watching. When I woke the next morning in the grey light outside it was silent; only the crows cried. I drank, peed and went back to bed. I still found the slightest movement exhausting. Lying in bed I felt nothing. There was no tension, no anxiety, no pain, only a great peaceful numbness. A little later I heard the rattle of Jack's door chain. I stumbled frantically onto the balcony.

'Jack!' I called. Jack was half way across the meadow, but he stopped and looked up, 'Jack, I'm ill,' I called down, 'I need a thermos flask. Can you get me one?'and I threw some money down to him.

Jack came back later that morning with my thermos and a fresh supply of limes. I was too tired to move and I called him into the room, but he was ill at ease and didn't stay long. With a thermos I could make a supply of hot lemon that would last the whole day. I drifted in and out of sleep. The day passed and the night came with more rain. The house was totally silent. The rats became bolder and scampered fearlessly around while I followed them with the beam of my torch. I lay powerless while they climbed around my table, gnawed at jar lids and ripped at food boxes.

The next morning after I had made my thermos of hot lemon I drank one glass and, to my astonishment, vomited. As I had not eaten for four days, my vomit was hot lemon, but suspended in it was a strange black slime. It smelt like old ash trays and was utterly foul. The effort of vomiting exhausted me and I slept until midday. When I awoke I drank a little more hot lemon but moments later threw it up. Shattered by the effort I again fell asleep. I now kept a bucket beside the urine filled jerry can. Their contents were too disgusting to simply empty over the edge of the balcony, and I was too weak to venture any further from the house. For the next three days this process continued. Between times I lay on my bed slipping in and out of sleep. Sometimes it would be daylight, sometimes night, but by now it made little difference. The rain came and went. The house was shrouded in silence. I only moved to fulfil my bodily functions, pissing, drinking and vomiting. I was utterly alone. I forgot about the other rooms in the house. They were empty. I forgot about the house, it too was empty. I forgot about the world beyond the cold raining mist, that too was empty. And slowly I became aware of death in the room, not too close but present as if by obligation, sitting by the window, watching me.

Finally the vomiting stopped. I began to stay awake longer and started to read again. A few more days passed. I lay in the quiet of my room and was strangely happy, filled with an unfamiliar peace. Then one morning I heard foot steps on the balcony and a tomboyish young woman pushed the door open and looked in.

'Hello,' she said with a strong Irish accent, 'are you Ken ? I've brought up your post from the village'

'Thanks,' I said.

'What are you doing in bed?' she asked, 'are you ill?'

'I'm much better now, but I have been ill. Very ill,' I said, noticing my speech, hearing the sound of each word, aware of the silence between the words.

'How long have you been here?'

'I'm not sure. I've lost track of time, but it must be about ten days now.'

'Ten days! Did you not see anyone?'

'Well, Jack brought me a thermos,' I said.

She shook her head in disbelief then came over nearer the bed and looked at me.

'By the colour of your face,' she said, 'I'd say you've got Hepatitis.'

She thought for a few moments.

'You can't stay here. We'll have to move you down to a hotel in the village and get you to the Tibetan doctor.'

She packed some of my clothes in a bag, and dismissed my apologies about the ghastly containers under my bed with the air of an experienced ward sister. I lay and watched her take things in hand, I noticed that I saw her clearly, that my mind was quiet in a way I had never experienced before. Yet as she moved around the room I saw my thoughts begin again to build descriptions. They came slowly at first, like fishes in a tank, floating through the silence. They began dividing the inner from the outer. The description and the described.

I spent two weeks at the Green Hotel. I visited Yeshi Dhondon, the Tibetan Doctor, who took my pulse, whisked up a sample of my urine in a jam jar with a chop stick and gave me herbal medicine. I was extremely weak and had to spend most of the day in bed. Joyce, the girl who had found me, came by to visit me one day, and said if I wanted to move back to Balcony house she and her partner would be happy to do my shopping. A couple of days later I packed my bag and, very slowly, made my way back to Balcony house. Joyce and her partner Michele had moved into Sally's old room next to mine. I had so little strength I spent most of my days just sitting on the balcony, reading or spacing out. Occasionally I would take a gentle walk around the hill, but even this mild exertion left me exhausted and needing a sleep. But I felt differently about myself. Some of the quietness I had experienced while I was ill remained with me. I could, for the first time in my life, easily sit and rest in a calm and quiet inner space. After years of self doubting, agitated insecurity I felt I had arrived. I was finally cool.

During the following weeks I began to experiment with meditation. I tried taking up the posture, and as Goenka had directed, started to observe the natural in and out flow of breath. Each time I did this, although I was sitting quite still, my body temperature suddenly began to rise. The longer I sat the hotter I became. I would strip off layer after layer of clothes until I sat in just a shirt, yet the moment I stopped paying attention to my breath my temperature fell, and I would have to put my clothes back on. So I did not meditate much, it was too uncomfortable. I just sat enjoying being contentedly spaced out. I started to wear white cotton clothes, and an old red shawl that I wrapped, monk like, over one shoulder. I pulled my long hair into a top knot and fancied I looked like one of the Nyingmas, an esoteric sect of Tibetan Yogis.

Laurie came back from Hunza and stayed a week in my room. We both were struck down with diarrhoea and spent most of the week in bed, which for Laurie was just his grimy sleeping bag on the floor. We talked and read, and every few hours ran out into the rain and leech infested grass to vacate our bowls.

'In a way,' I said, as I told him about my illness, 'I realised there is no security, and that in knowing that insecurity I have found the only true security.'

Laurie moved back to Glenmore. By now I had run out of money and was living on what I had managed to borrow. In a month my old friends, Jess and Helen, would be coming to India. I wrote to my parents and asked them if they could give Jess and Helen some money for me. In my letter I tried to explain that I was on a spiritual journey, that I had to stay in India, that the idea of going back was now unthinkable. As the arrival date of Jess and Helen drew close I became uneasy. I felt as if they were part of another life that belonged to someone else. They had known the old insecure Ken, and I wondered if they would appreciate the new, cool one.

Finally the day came when they arrived, panting onto the meadow in front of Balcony house. They looked dreadfully like three-month tourists. They came up to my room and unpacked their stuff. After the penniless existence I had been living it was strange to see their cameras, the bird watching binoculars and all their new and clean things. They had brought my silver flute, which had arrived safely back through the post, and a hundred pounds in cash from my parents. Once they had unpacked we decided to walk to McLeod for chai. Just as we were leaving I stuffed the cash into an old tin among my food storage jars. I locked the door with my padlock, a cheap tinny one from the bazaar, which until then, because I had no money nor anything of value, I had hardly bothered to use. When we returned a few hours later the padlock was broken, and Jess and Helen's cameras, binoculars and film had gone. So had my flute. Helen began to cry. It was not a good start.

As I had feared, the forest dwelling pseudo Nyingma Yogi that I believed I had become was not very comfortable with Jess and Helen. On top of that they had come to the squalor of Balcony house in the monsoon. It was cold, damp and the floor in my room was lumpy and uncomfortable. The fleas, which by now hardly affected me, tormented them, covering them in red lumps. Nothing seemed to go right and my happy, damp solitude was full of awkward silences. We were almost strangers, but I could not go back, I stuck to the new script, the new self.

A German woman, who was studying Tibetan medicine, was making a trip up beyond Triund to collect medicinal herbs. She lived an austere life in a one roomed hut on the meadow behind Balcony house. Jess and Helen decided to accompany her. On the day the three of them left the monsoon set in again. I suddenly became tired of the cold, damp forest and, as I could now afford it, I packed a bag and moved down to the Green Hotel. Three days later Jess and Helen returned, totally shattered. The cave in which they stayed had turned out to be little more than a rock overhang. It had rained continuously, and they had spent most of the day and night clutching their sleeping bags trying to avoid the water that poured through cracks in the rock above them. They stayed a night at the Green Hotel, then moved down to the Tibetan Library.

In September the monsoon finally began to break up. It was two months since I had gone down with Hepatitis, and although I was still weak, I was much recovered. After a week at the Green Hotel where I enjoyed the luxury of eating all three meals out and taking hot showers, I moved up to Glenmore and lived on the veranda there, something I would not have dared to do before. I felt free. I had dropped all plans to go back to England. I was a free spirit in India, a yogi, a spiritual seeker who had left all behind for a life on the road. I travelled light, a small bag, a rolled up sleeping bag, tied with an Indian scarf. I had a small chillum and my stash of hashish. I was no longer a six month tourist, I had gone up a caste, I belonged, I felt at home. I had gained a promotion on the ladder of self improvement.

I wanted to do a long meditation retreat, not a ten day guided course, but a serious long solitude, alone for months, where I could explore the outer limits of my coolness. So I wrote to the Goenka centre near Bombay asking if I could stay there for several months. I also wanted to travel again, so I decided to visit Solpema. Solpema was where Padma Sambhava had lived. He was the great Tantric master, who in the eighth century introduced Tantric teachings to Tibet. The story went that while living at Solpema he had acquired the daughter of a local King as a disciple. When the king discovered his daughter was living with a hermit in a cave he was so enraged he set off with his troops to deal with the upstart. He arrested the totally unmoved Padma Sambhava and threw his daughter into a pit of thorns. He then built a great pyre in order to burn the hermit alive. The great Guru waited until he was on top of the burning pyre then, using his Tantric powers, turned the whole area into a beautiful lake upon which he and his consort floated on a throne of lotus petals. The lake was still there.

It took a day by bus to get there. It was strange after eight months living in McLeod to be travelling. I found I was very at ease with India. I no longer felt like a tourist. Solpema turned out to be a tiny, windswept village perched on the edge of a barren hillside. There were no other westerners, no hotels and only one beat up chai shop that served rice and dal. I was given a room at the Tibetan temple beside the lake which nestled improbably into the hill side. That night as I sat in the complete silence of my bare room, a small voice in me began again, quiet but insistent, to ask the same old questions: Why are you here? Where does this all lead? What will become of you? I pushed the thoughts away. I was through with all that. I was not fearful or confused. I was a traveller, a yogi, a pilgrim. I was cool.

I visited the cave hermitages, and had tea with a lama and his western pupil. I visited the sacred caves where a thirty-foot gold statue of Padma Sambhava filled a dark fissure in the hillside. Several times a day I walked around the lake, enjoying the shade of the trees that grew at its edge. On one of these walks, as I passed through the village, a mangy old bazaar dog joined me. We walked together for the afternoon. When I stopped for tea, she waited patiently outside the chai shop, so I took her out a bread roll. The following morning she greeted me on the street, tail wagging. I fed her, and she would not leave my side throughout the day. When I sat in the shade of trees, she lay at my feet and I stroked her worn and hairless back. The next day when, I came to leave, she waited with me at the bus stand surrounded by a bustling crowd of Zanskarie nomads on pilgrimage. When the bus arrived, as usual everyone rushed for the door at once. I allowed myself to be carried onto the bus and found a seat. The dog hung back, afraid of the crowd and the machine. Then with a jolt the bus began to move. Looking back I saw her take a few hesitant steps after the vehicle, but she stopped and sat down in the middle of the road. She just sat there and watched the bus go. I watched her dwindle away, smaller and smaller until the dust cloud swallowed her up.

In Mandi I spent my days by the fast flowing river with the

Sadhus and Yogis. In my tatty lungi, long hair and scraggy beard I felt I was almost one of them. Then from Mandi I caught the bus up the long gorge that led to the Kulu valley. I was heading for Manali, a tourist town at the head of the valley. In Manali I met up again with Jess and Helen. We travelled together over the Rhotang pass, one of the few high passes in the Himalayas with a metalled road. On the far side was Zanskar, more part of Tibet than India. We went to Keylang, the largest town, and found a village with old canvas tents that provided crude lodgings for visiting Indian administrators and the odd tourist. All the flat land was man made, terraced fields that stepped down the steep mountain sides around the few towns and villages. The only trees were lines of poplars clinging to the banks of water courses. As it was autumn the leaves were turning vivid gold, the only colour in a landscape of infinite browns. Far below, rivers of churning brown water cut through the landscape, sawing through the rock on their way to the Indian plains. The people had Mongolian features, and their religion was Buddhism.

In Keylang I heard about an Englishman who lived up the valley in a tiny Zanskari village, and spent the winter in a cave high in the snow bound mountains. I knew it had to be Stacy, and even though it was rather late in the day I set out to visit him. The day was almost over when I began the final steep climb up to the village, which was little more than a hamlet, a jumble of deserted stone buildings. As I entered between the houses I came upon Stacy. He had had his hair cropped, and was wearing an old leather coat tied at the waist, ragged shorts and very worn green canvas Indian army boots. He was standing in the street amiably berating an old Zanskari woman who was looking at the ground sheepishly. To emphasise what he was saying he tapped her several times on the arm with his stick. A cloud of dust rose from the layers of never washed clothing she wore. He had the wry smile of an elder talking to a small naughty child. When he saw me he broke off and spoke in English.

'Hello! Come on up, you must be thirsty, I'll make some tea.'

After parting with the old woman we walked together up through the village.

'What was going on there?' I asked.

'Oh,' he said, 'I've been asking them to sell me some wool. I need to make a pullover for the winter, but they tell me to buy some in the bazaar. They know as well as I do that all you can get in the bazaar is synthetic rubbish. It just isn't warm enough.'

Stacy held a position here. He had helped build a temple in the village, carrying rocks up the mountain on his back. He also spent the winters alone in a cave, something the locals would never do. In fact, because of the road to Manali, they no longer even spent the winters in the village. The road had meant new markets for their potato crops, which meant cash, and cash meant they could now spend the winter in the comparative comfort of Manali.

Stacy's room was sparse. While the water boiled on the small stove we sat in silence. Outside the room there was no sound at all and the silence seemed to penetrate the whole room. Stacy began to mix up some grass for a chillum. Then he made some tea and sat by the window looking out.

'How are things in Glenmore these days?' he asked.

I passed on various bits of news.

'They are all so crazy,' he said, 'but you do have to admire them.'

'I received a letter from Jessica,' he told me with enthusiasm, taking out from an inner pocket an incredibly worn letter, almost in pieces, 'she's staying in a monastery in Dhera Dun, she seems to be well.'

As we sat there the effects of the chillum began to work. The silence was so intense it seemed too much to bear. It seemed to press in on the illusory self I had created. Stacy, Jessica, were beings who inhabited a consciousness I believed must be quite different from mine. I began to feel afraid. Afraid to be seen. Afraid that I would be seen as I really was.

'Pity you didn't bring your sleeping bag,' Stacy said amiably, 'but I'm sure I can rustle up some bedding.'

My heart was beating hard. The thought of having to sit with this man, hiding my fear for a whole evening, suddenly seemed appalling.

'I've made plans to leave tomorrow with my friends,' I lied with a mixture of fear and shame, 'I really should get back tonight.'

'Okay,' said Stacy easily.

We sat for a while longer, then he began to prepare another mound of grass for a chillum.

'I don't think I can handle smoking that,' I said, 'I do have to be able get back,' my false laughter hung in the air.

'Okay,' he said, again with the same ease, putting the grass and chillum to one side. I wanted to stay. I wanted to be able to talk to him. To find out how he could live with the silence, how he could live with this vast aloneness. I wanted to know what he knew, yet I could not ask. I was running away, hiding my fear from his inscrutable gaze.

'Right then,' he said getting up, 'we'd better get you back to town.'

We set off back through the village. On the far side we came to the newly built temple, which was still bare stone.

'We will let the stones settle for a year before putting plaster on the walls,' Stacy informed me.

Looking through the gap in the door I could see, in the yellow light of butter lamps, a ten foot golden statue of a Padma

Sambhava.

'We believe that he stayed here on his way to Tibet,' he said. I wondered if he had stayed in the cave where Stacy spent the winter. He led me around the dark corridor of prayer wheels that ran around the inner shrine. He went at an alarming speed. On the last wall, as he span the rickety wheels, one fell out of its mountings.

'A bad omen?' I enquired jokingly.

'I don't believe in any of that pseudo religious rubbish,' he answered curtly.

When we came out I staggered around, my head spinning from the darkness and turning wheels. Stacy laughed, 'this way,' he said, and he led me down a zigzag path at a speed I could only just keep up with. We wound down the steep hill-side at a steady half run until we reached the road. It was still a three mile walk to Keylang. He walked to the outskirts of town with me, chatting amiably as we walked. There he stopped. It was by now completely dark.

'I'll leave you here then,' he said holding out his hand.

We shook hands, then he turned and strode off into the darkness.

A couple of weeks later I arrived back in McLeod. It was a wonderful feeling to come back, being recognised and greeted by the shop keepers, the chai shop owners and even the young leprous beggar who lived near the temple. At Glenmore Joan was sitting on the veranda inspecting her belly. She had practised a Tibetan method of birth control, wearing around her waist a thin red cord which had been blessed and empowered by a Lama. Now she had had to cut the cord, because she was pregnant.

We talked and smoked and I told her that I had met Stacy.

'He's like a saint,' I said, my admiration spilling out .

'Well,' scoffed Joan, 'there's saints and there's sinners.'

I stayed two nights at Glenmore. Joan invited me to sleep in her room. As we prepared for bed and I got into my sleeping bag on the floor, she sat upright in her bed and smiled broadly across at me.

I smiled back. 'Goodnight,' I said.

She snorted and turned off the light.

In the darkness I realised she had been inviting me to her bed.

The next day I planned to visit Joyce and Michele and spend the night at Balcony house. By the late afternoon I had my bag packed, but I couldn't bring myself to leave. Twice I wandered off into the woods, but each time it was as if an invisible cord was pulling me back, and I returned rather sheepishly to the veranda. Then Laurie arrived.

'That's why you couldn't leave!' cried Joan.

Laurie had a letter for me from the Goenka centre at Igatpuri, which he had noticed at Poste-restante and already opened.

'Letters from Dharmagiri I consider public property,' he told me.

The letter said that, as I had only sat one course with Goenka, they recommended I sit another course led by him before embarking on a long period of meditation alone. The next one was to be in Jaipur, Rajasthan. Laurie was planning to go, and we decided to travel down to Delhi together. The next afternoon we caught the night bus to Delhi. Once we were out of the hills the road was straight and flat, the bus fast and empty. It was too bumpy to sleep, instead Laurie rolled a steady stream of small joints. We sat side by side, our bags stuffed under the seats, cocooned in a dim, yellow lit missile of rattling windows, hurtling through a black void. We talked all through the night. It was good to have a friend.

Chapter 6

There were two weeks until the meditation courses in Jaipur. Laurie wanted to go to the camel fair in Pushkar, the place where I had been bitten by a street dog. I had no great urge to go back there, and I wanted to visit the Taj Mahal. Leaving my rucksack with the hotel in Delhi, I set off for Agra with a shoulder bag, bed roll and flute. I spent a few days in Agra visiting the Taj and other sights. In a guide book I discovered there was a bird sanctuary near the town of Bharatpur. Bahratpur was halfway between Agra and Jaipur. Imagining somewhere quiet and green, I decided to spend the remaining few days there before the meditation course began.

I had expected to be met at Bharatpur bus station with cries of, 'You want cheap hotel! You want see birds! You come with me!' but instead there was a barren, oily yard where sun blackened peasants viewed me with passive curiosity.

I asked a passer by, 'Bird sanctuary?'

'You want go Bird sanctuary? You go that way.'

He pointed to a road leading out of town.

'Is it far?' I asked.

'No, not far,' he replied, which meant anything between ten minutes and a three hour walk. I set off, bed roll across my back, feeling uneasy.

I had left the town far behind by the time I reached the entrance to the sanctuary. It looked like the entrance to an industrial estate that had never been built. There was just a gate way and a bit of wall. To my surprise a little man came out of a hut and told me I would have to pay to enter. I paid and continued walking. There was no difference to the landscape. After half an hour I was beginning to wonder if there was anywhere to walk to. Just then I saw another westerner, a young attractive woman in shorts and T shirt, strolling towards me. When we came face to face I smiled and she smiled back.

'Is there anywhere I can stay here?' I asked.

'Oh yes,' she said, speaking with a Scandinavian accent, 'just walk another hundred metres and you will come to the Tourist Lodge.'

She pointed to a bend in the road ahead.

The Lodge was a modern building, with large, plate glass windows, designed to suit the needs of what Indian officials would call 'bona fide' tourists. I took a seat in the pretentious but slightly tatty lounge. It was peopled by middle aged western tourists festooned with camera equipment. Uniformed waiters hovered around the edge of the room. It could have been a continent, rather than a few kilometres, from Bahratpur. I felt self-conscious with my hair pulled into a top knot, scruffy Indian clothes and luggage of shoulder bag and bed roll. The young woman from the road came in and walked over to where I sat.

'Can I join you?' she asked, sitting down. The khaki shorts she was wearing displayed her smooth brown legs. She crossed them, accentuating the curve of her thigh. I was not used to such legs.

'You walked all the way from the town?' she asked.

'Yes, I didn't know what to expect here,' I replied.

'You are interested in birds?' she asked.

'Well, not particularly. I just happened to be passing this way,' I replied.

'Well,' she said warmly, 'let me get you something to drink. You must be thirsty.'

She ordered a lemon soda from one of the waiters.

'And you,' I asked, 'how did you come here?'

'I am with a tour from Denmark. We are all bird watchers. I am the group doctor, and mostly the rest of the group are ill,' she laughed conspiratorially, 'I have been trekking in Nepal before coming here. It was so beautiful, I want to go back and live there.'

She frowned as if this thought troubled her.

'Sometimes I think that I would be running away, wanting to escape from my problems.'

'Well,' I suggested, 'if a problem goes away by escaping from it, then you haven't got a problem anymore,' this advice did not sound quite right.

'Do you think so?' she asked.

As we talked she kept nervously tangling and untangling her legs which made my stomach nervously knot and unknot in response.

Suddenly she jumped up, looking at her watch.

'I have to go to lunch with the group now. I am sorry I cannot invite you to eat with us, but it is all included in our tour,' she shrugged apologetically and went to join her group who were now gathered at a long table. They were doing their best not to stare at us.

I still hadn't seen any sign of anything that looked remotely like a bird sanctuary. Feeling rather foolish, like someone in a library unable to find the books, I asked one of the young Indian staff where the birds in this bird sanctuary were. He pointed to a small path between the bushes just outside the guest house. Walking between the bushes I found myself almost immediately on a tree lined causeway. Still water stretched out on both sides, the surface of the water was broken only by reeds and lone trees. I wandered along enjoying the shade and tranquillity. The edge of the sanctuary was a wide bank, a thirty-foot-wide dike, dotted with mature trees. On one side there was a dusty and waterless landscape, on the other a sanctuary of shade, water and trees. The causeway crossed the sanctuary which was only a few hundred yards wide. I followed the path on between large trees and soon came to a village. The villagers gathered in their doorways and watched me. A man shouted and beckoned me over. With elaborate formality I was asked to sit on a rug that had been spread out on the small earth veranda in front the houses. The children pushed and shoved, crowding the narrow alley outside the house, trying to get a look at the weird visitor. A woman placed a stainless steel tray in front of me. There were several thick chapattis and a small bowl of unidentifiable green vegetables swimming in oil, red with chillies. The food was cold but the chillies burnt like hot coals in my mouth, making my eyes water. I was given a stainless steel cup of what looked like watery milk. I drank deeply to cool my mouth to find it was incredibly salty; it was like drinking milk flavoured sea water.

'Good?' he asked.

'Mmm! Very good!' I lied, hopelessly burning out the salty taste with more chilli. Once I had eaten my host pointed to his watch.

'Duty,' he said, 'Factory.'

I insisted on paying him for the food, but it was the wrong thing to do and it embarrassed him.

'Please,' I said misguidedly, 'buy some sweets for the children.'

He held the money up and declared loudly for all to hear, to exonerate his acceptance, 'for sweets! for the children!'

As I walked back to the sanctuary, three grubby kids followed me along the causeways. One girl was carrying her baby sister. When I stopped for a rest they crowded around me. Pointing at the baby's tiny rib cage, the girl began to whimper pitifully. With little conviction they poked their begging palms at me. They were not fooled by my wandering yogi look; they saw my white skin and knew it meant cash. Still feeling indebted for my meal I looked in my wallet, and found I only had a twenty rupee note. It was an absurdly large amount, but I could not bring myself to turn them away. So I gave it to the oldest girl. Laughing nervously, she tucked the money inside her blouse, and ran for it before I could change my mind.

I came upon a young man watching his water buffalo graze in the shallows. He called me over. I spent the afternoon with him, smoking beedies and struggling to communicate with my bad Hindi. He was a thoughtful young man, unusually interested in where I came from, and how things were for me there. As the sun set his buffalo made their way back to him, grazing their way through the shallow water. We walked back towards his village together and parted affectionately. Back near the guest house I sat on a pier and watched the sun set over the water. The orange sky was full of birds returning to roost for the night, they merged into the water bound trees, black on black in the twilight. The staff at the New Tourist Lodge let me sleep in the foyer of the old bungalow next door. I made a bed on the floor with cushions from the arm chairs. The next morning I took a long walk around the sanctuary and watched the sun rise. Back at the lodge the waiters invited me over, gave me breakfast and refused payment. The doctor came swooping in, all legs and flowing hair. She came over smiling, and asked if I had slept well.

'I have to go to my group for breakfast now, we have our morning meeting,' she said.

They had already gathered at the long breakfast table, like a ghastly collection of chaperones, and I could hear them discussing their recent bowel movements. I was ready to go. I thanked the waiters, swung my bed roll over my shoulder and headed off down the road. It was already hot, and I had a long walk back to Bahratpur.

After a mile or so I came upon a small white temple at the side of the road. It was a shabby little place, thick with a thousand layers of peeling white wash. Sitting outside was a tiny, very thin, old Baba dressed in the rags of a Sadhu. He called out and beckoned me over, patting the ground next to him. He was preparing a heap of ganja for a chillum. He made it all ready, but then offered it to me. He insisted I smoke it all. Once I had finished he made another chillum for himself. He showed little further interest in me, so I just sat with him in the morning sun waiting for something to happen. A rather earnest looking man with long hair and a beard, wearing orange cotton clothes, arrived on a bicycle. Rajindra Singh had come to visit his Guru and he spoke English. The Guru showed as little interest in Rajindra as he had in me. Rajindra began to question me in the usual way.

'From which country are you coming?'

'What is the purpose of your visit?'

'Are you in public service or private business?'

'Are you married?'

I began to try to explain I was a traveller. I was on my way to do a meditation course. Had he heard of Goenka?

'This Goenka is your Guru?' enthused Rajindra, 'so you also have a Guru! This is my Guru,' he pointed to the old Baba, 'he is very wise, I am coming here every day.' I looked at the almost catatonic old Baba who seemed to have forgotten we were there. Rajindra continued to question me, 'so you have been to university?'

'Well no, I went to art school.'

'So you are an artist then?' he asked.

'I suppose so,' I replied.

'Could you paint a holy picture on the wall of our temple?' asked Rajindra enthusiastically.

'Well, yes I could but...' I hesitated, as I was not entirely comfortable with the look on Rajindra's face.

'I must ask my Guru if he is agreeable to my idea,' Rajindra told me without bothering to ask if I was agreeable to his idea.

He turned and began to speak to the Baba who showed no apparent awareness that he was now the object of Rajindra's attention. Rajindra was full of devotional humility and treated the old man with great respect. As Rajindra spoke the old Guru's milky, glazed eyes wandered vaguely in my direction but then, as if deciding that Rajindra and I did not warrant even that degree of interest, just nodded barely perceptibly and continued to stare into the middle distance.

'He has agreed!' Rajindra cried triumphantly.

'Rajindra, I will need to go to the bazaar and get materials if I am to do the picture.'

'I will take you!' he said leaping up, 'but first you must come to my house.'

With a sinking heart I found myself perched painfully on the cross bar of his bike, trapped between his arms, wobbling down the road to Bahratpur.

It turned out he was not a homeless wanderer, but had a small weaving business. He put on his orange pyjamas when he visited his Guru, and his impressively long hair and beard were because he was a Sikh. He was a fake Yogi like me. In a back room he showed me two ancient mechanical looms from which he managed to make a living with his two sons. His wife, he told me, had died fifteen years earlier, and he had never remarried. In the bare downstairs room he had set up a bed platform covered in a white sheet. It was a holy man's teaching podium. This was where every day, he told me with pride, he read the scriptures. He sat on the edge of the bed and asked me to come up and sit with him. He called loudly for his sons to come and meet his guest.

They entered, young men rather than boys, and sullenly

stood by the door, watching me mistrustfully. Rajindra introduced me to them in Hindi. I could not understand what he was saying, but when he had finished he made a command, which he had to repeat loudly and sternly. The two boys shuffled over to me, muttering resentfully, and casting me hateful looks bent down and kissed my feet. I froze, horrified.

'Now my sons will take you to the bazaar to buy your painting materials,' Rajindra told me.

When I returned I found Rajindra's brother, who lived next door, had invited us to his house for lunch. Once the formalities were over, he took me into his little shrine room and began to give me a potted, five-thousand-year history of Hinduism, introducing me to each new God with enthusiasm. His explanations of the scriptures were simplistic, blindly devotional and tedious. As time went on I found that whatever aspect of Hinduism he was describing, he managed always to bring the conclusion to what awful people the Muslims were. At first it was amusing because it was so obvious, but it quickly stopped being funny.

'We Hindu people are very clean because we are taught in our religion to wash every day, but these Muslim people are dirty people, they are not washing,' he looked at me nodding seriously.

'But surely Muslims also wash!' I complained, 'I know Muslim people wash. I have lived with them.'

'No! You are wrong, they do not wash, they are dirty,' he said emphatically.

'In their mosques they kick our holy books around on the floor,' he said with conviction.

'Surely not...' I said, but he was not interested in my defence of Muslims.

'That is not the only thing they are doing. They also sacrifice goats by cutting their throats slowly,' he waited for my exclamation of horror, and when none came he continued, 'they marry their own sisters, they steal also....' and his hate filled litany went on and on in a loud and insistent voice. My heart sank and I began to feel slightly panicky. It was so stupid, so ugly, that suddenly I could take it no longer.

'You have convinced me!' I blurted out with mad irony, 'all Muslims are bad people. You have shown me. You are right. Now I hate all Muslim people. I understand now that all Muslim people are bad, dirty, cruel, greedy, violent, stupid and ignorant. You have shown me the facts. Now I understand.'

He was silent for a few seconds, and looked a little shocked. Then he smiled the smile of one amused by those who are ignorant of the obvious, and continued his lecture.

After lunch and some loud displays of scripture reading by both Rajindra and his brother, we returned to the temple. The Guru was still squatting outside, his boney knees up by his chin and a cigarette dangling from his lips. I worked away during the afternoon painting a green Tara, the goddess of compassion, on the temple wall. Neither Rajindra nor the Guru seemed to care much what I painted, as long as it was a deity. The light ran out before I had finished and I was doomed to return to Rajindra's house. I was dreading meeting his brother and, sure enough, he appeared and began again in a loud voice his bigoted diatribe. I resigned myself; he was too mad and stupid, it was not worth arguing with him. We ate supper together while he explained how religious Hindus were about food, and how pure the food was and what good Hindus they were, how they lived a religious life. After supper Rajindra moved a charpoy into his room as a bed for me. Then he went and sat on his white covered podium and began again to read loudly from the scriptures. I fell asleep as his voice droned on and on.

The next day I finished my mural. Underneath I wrote a verse I had found and copied in my diary.

They reckon ill who leave me out
When me they fly, I am the wings
I am the doubter and the doubt
and I am the hymn the Brahman sings.

I had one last meal at Rajindra's. We went upstairs to his bedroom, a desolate, brick shack on the roof of the house. In one corner there was an old charpoy, but the rest of the room was like a derelict farm shed. There were a few dust covered pots on shelves, thick with dirt. There was no door and only holes for windows. It was a desolate place and suddenly I wanted to save him from his lonely life, his sadness, the wife he had lost, the cruel and stupid brother who dominated him.

'Come to Jaipur with me and sit the meditation course with Goenka,' I said, 'there are no charges, you are only asked to give a donation equal to your means. It is entirely voluntary.'

'I am not sure I would be able not to eat anything after noon,' he said doubtfully.

'Of course you would!' I insisted, 'it really is not difficult.'

But Rajindra didn't want to come.

'I already have a Guru,' he said.

I boarded the bus to Jaipur with a great sense of relief. The bus was nearly empty, but sitting at the back, like naughty schoolboys, were two grubby, Italian hippies. I went and sat a few seats in front of them. As we hurtled at top speed across the dusty countryside one of them rolled a joint and passed it over to me.

I arrived at the Jaipur meditation centre with two meditators I had met at the Jaipur youth hostel. One was Dieter, an earnest young German medical student. He had sat several meditation courses in Europe and had come to India to meditate with Goenka. Dieter was irritatingly keen on the whole business. The other was Palinko, a laid-back Yugoslavian who was studying mathematics at the university in Delhi. He was new to meditation. The meditation centre was in a desert valley several miles outside Jaipur. The whole valley was a sacred place, and on the way in we passed many small temples and shrines. The centre was at the far end of the valley. There was a recently completed meditation hall. Next to it was a pagoda with a circle of cells in the same style as the centre at Igatpuri. The rest of the site was dotted with gaily striped tents giving the appearance of an Ottoman army camp. Peacocks wandered around the small sandy knolls and flowering desert bushes. The bare sand and rocky hills were silent and starkly defined by a rich blue sky.

That evening, nine months after my first course, I found myself nervously waiting to enter a meditation hall for my second ten days of silent sitting meditation. I was already irritated by the structure and regimentation of the place. I was not sure I liked being herded around, obeying rules, sticking to a time table. After the spiritual anarchy of Mcleod, where the path to enlightenment could encompass a long afternoon hanging out on the veranda at Glenmore smoking a few chillums, the notices, 'Male area only. No bathing during meditation periods. Please keep Noble silence during meal times....' were all a bit much. Yet as I waited to enter the hall I was afraid. I was afraid that once I sat alone in the cell with only my own mind for company I might just find I was not the person I liked to think I had become.

The course began as before, with three days of Anapana meditation, observation of the breath. As before, when I allowed my mind to wander I found I could easily sit through the hour-long sessions. I could even manage an hour in the full lotus position. I dreamed away the hours as a perfect imitation Buddha, and I began to feed the resentment I felt at being shut up in a dark room with a lot of suffering pious Indians. I told myself I was beyond this, this nose-to-the-grind-stone approach to liberation.

'You have to work,' Goenka kept telling us, 'no one else can work for you. Work and you are bound to be successful.'

The days passed by and my resentment grew. I looked at the Indians sitting the course and decided they were all rich men attempting to ease their guilty lives with a bit of religion. I turned my growing anger onto Goenka, and it became obvious to me he was a charlatan. A man lost on a massive ego trip. His style of chanting, the absurdly deep voice, seemed so pretentious I was sure, at any moment, he was about to crack. I waited for him to break down in front of us all, unable to carry on the charade. I disregarded his Vipassana meditation instructions as I had disregarded the Anapana instructions. It seemed a waste of time when I could sit cross legged so comfortably spacing out. So I continued to space out at great length, recreating my past and constructing in great detail improbably happy futures.

Every few days we were called in groups to the front of the hall for a checking session. We sat in a line and Goenka questioned each one of us, like a dignitary meeting the work force.

'You get sensations, Hmm? Yes? Good. Keep moving the attention around the body.'

Then to the next.

'You get sensations? Good. Keep moving the attention around the body.'

We were told to treat pain as another sensation, or if the mind wandered too much, to come back to breath awareness. Once he had reached the end of the line he asked us to sit with him for a few moments meditating. Then he would dismiss us with a smile saying, 'Good, good, keep working...'

It was on the fifth day that I noticed Palinko. He was wandering around staring into the middle distance, looking pretty crazy. During the afternoon's session of strong determination meditation, the hour long sitting without moving, Palinko suddenly got up, came to the front of the hall and began a series of elaborate prostration's at Goenka's feet. Goenka smiled and chuckled like some one being given an unexpected present.

'Hmm, please,' he said benignly, raising one hand slightly, 'return to your seat, hmm?'

I was appalled at the way he accepted this show of devotion when it was clear Palinko was seriously off his trolley. Each time I saw Palinko he was looking worse and worse. I wanted to do something, but found I had an irrational desire not to break my silence. I had decided that if I could stay for the whole ten days, keeping the silence and sitting on my cushion, I would be able to make a definitive judgement about whether or not it was the path for me. I could then say I had given it a fair trail, I would be able to put it behind me and could get on with my life. And I had such a wonderful life ahead of me, I had honed it down to perfection during the endless hours of day dreaming. Finally an American, who was sharing the same dormitory tent as Palinko, and knew we had arrived together, approached me.

'Your friend is in a bad way,' he said, 'I don't think he has eaten for the past four days.'

I felt quite cross at this intrusion into my silence. I only had a few more days to go before I was through with it all and now this. I found Palinko standing, leaning slightly forward, eyes blank, staring into the distance.

'Palinko,' I asked, 'are you OK?'

He turned to me. His cracked lips moved into a mad smile, but he said nothing. My resentment dissolved.

'You had better come with me,' I told him, but he seemed not to hear me.

I took him by the hand, like a small child, and he followed me to the dining tent. An Indian doctor involved in the running of the course came and examined him. Palinko sat passively, staring through us, as we milled around discussing him.

'He is suffering from dehydration,' said the doctor, 'he must be given warm tea to drink.'

Palinko refused the tea, woodenly ignoring the offered cup, but finally, after much insistence he swallowed a small sip. The moment he swallowed his stomach spasmed and the tea came straight back up. The doctor looked worried.

'He will have to go to hospital,' he announced.

It was clear someone would have to go with him, but I did not want to go with this half crazy man alone into Jaipur general hospital. So I went and found Dieter. I told him what had happened, and he reluctantly agreed to come with me to the hospital. We were taken by one of the centre's founder members in his car. He was a wealthy man, and he made it clear he did not appreciate having Goenka's annual visit disrupted by troublesome young westerners.

We arrived at Jaipur hospital casualty department. Palinko was wheeled into the bare reception area and left on an old trolley bed. Finally a doctor came and gave him a large injection, a moment later Palinko slipped into a deep sleep. He was then put on a drip of Glucose water and was wheeled from casualty to a general ward. The ward was ghastly, a large room with ten beds on each side. The beds were grey with dirt and occupied by sprawled and emaciated dying bodies. At the far end were toilets and a washing area. The white ceramic sink was dark brown with dribbles of phlegm and betel juice. The walls were greasy and smeared with years of filth. The Indian style toilet was blocked and full with a mound of turds. Urine and excrement were overflowing out into the hall. People had shit on the floor rather than onto the stinking heap. A group of young doctors walked through on their rounds. They were wearing immaculate white coats, holding clip boards and seemed oblivious to their surroundings.

Dieter and I stayed through the evening and night with Palinko. The glucose water sachets, four litres in all, emptied slowly into his body. The night was punctuated by bouts of violent tubercular coughing and groans. In the early hours the dead body of one patient was removed, and another was brought to the same bed without changing it's grey filthy sheet. Dieter and I had put a mattress on the floor next to Palinko's bed, but it was hard to sleep on the same level as the unemptied spittoons and toilet floors. Dieter and I talked about the course. I expressed my misgivings about Vipassana meditation, but Dieter would not talk about my doubts. He kept giving me the party line, everything is craving and all is impermanent, and by the morning I wanted to get away from him. I wanted to resolve my doubts, and felt that the interruption in the course had stopped me from achieving this. I knew there was to be a three day course between the two ten day courses, and I decided I would go and join it.

Palinko had returned to his right mind by the morning.

'Why did you do it?' I asked him.

He shook his head and replied, 'I don't know, I don't know.'

It was not a very reassuring answer.

Dieter and I moved Palinko out of the Hospital to the youth hostel where we had originally met. I told Dieter I wanted to return to the centre to sit the three day course.

'But I also wish to sit the three day course,' he told me.

'Well, one of us has to stay with Palinko, and as you believe everything is attachment and desire, this will be a good opportunity for you to practise it.'

This was entirely unfair, but Dieter, trapped by his own dogma, could do nothing but agree to stay.

That evening while I sat in a large, unfurnished hall at the hotel playing my flute enjoying the acoustics, Laurie walked in, just back from Pushkar. He was also planning to sit the three day course. The next morning when I picked up my post at the G.P.O I found a confused and unhappy letter from Eva in Sweden, with a bank draft for two hundred rupees. There was also a letter from my father. I had written to him again. I had spoken grandly of a spiritual journey, that India was my university. Ideas that now seemed rather false, as during the previous day's meditation the tone of my fantasies for my future in India had been pretty hedonistic, involving beautiful girls, sex, hashish and beaches, all experienced in an incredibly cool laid-back sort of way. Not the basis on which I had asked for my father's money. His letter was extraordinarily supportive.

'Money has never brought me any particular happiness,' he said, 'and if you can use it to find a lasting and more meaningful happiness then I am glad to give it.'

The same evening I went with Laurie back to the meditation centre and joined the three day course. As before, although I sat on the cushion, I made little effort to practice the meditation technique. During the first two days my resistance returned with a vengeance, and it began to boil up in me. I watched Goenka with growing distaste and resentment. I began to tone up my fantasies for the future. I could see myself with the beautiful people in Goa, and I thought how glad I would be to escape from the meditation camp and the pious middle class merchants sitting the course. In my diary I wrote, filled with hubris; 'Brahma dances in bliss, and I dance with him!'

On the final morning of the course we all gathered in the hall for 'Metta' meditation, the meditation on loving kindness. Goenka explained how we were to share feelings of loving compassion. First we should fill our hearts with love and forgiveness, forgiving anyone who had wronged us, and asking forgiveness from those we had wronged. Then we should feel love for all those in the hall, then spread our love out and out, to take in all being everywhere.

'What absurd nonsense!' I raged to myself, as Goenka began his lamentful Metta chanting, 'what false theatrics!'

Yet Goenka's chanting seemed to be pushing in against my resisting mind. Suddenly I couldn't bear it. Before I knew what I was doing I had struggled to my feet and walked out of the hall.

I waited outside for the end of session. I couldn't take in what I had done. When everyone came out, the silence was over and I went to find Laurie. We sat together among the dunes, looking out over the camp.

'How was your course?' I asked him.

'It was pretty strong,' he said seriously, 'how about you?'

This was what I had been waiting for and I launched into my critique of it all. I was in the middle of my tirade, being extravagantly rude about the 'pious merchants in dhotis,' when Laurie turned to me.

'If you could only hear yourself,' he said simply.

I did, and it was awful. It was posturing, arrogant and hateful. Worst of all, I knew all the rest was make believe. It was all just images. This was truth. The cool Yogi traveller burst like a balloon. Then I knew what stood between me and peace of mind.

'I think I need to see Goenkaji,' I said shakily.

Laurie looked up at me surprised, unaware of the devastating effect of his words.

'I think he's meeting people in the hall,' he said helpfully.

I waited my turn outside the hall. After a few minutes I was called in. I sat cross legged on the carpet in front of Goenka. He smiled down at me. He seemed to be radiating a warm love, so strong I could feel it soaking into me.

'I want to apologise to you,' I said, and as I spoke I felt so sad, so ashamed, that I began to cry, 'the last days here,' I sobbed, 'I have been throwing so much anger and hatred at you, and all the people here, who have organised this course, who have fed me and made all this possible, and I want to say I am sorry.'

Goenka chuckled affectionately.

'No need to apologise!' he said smiling, 'that is our job! That is what I am here for! And the others, they understand that deep Sankaras of hatred and anger come up. It is good, the mind is purifying itself.' And he laughed a warm friendly laugh. I laughed with him and cried at the same time.

'What should I do?' I asked,' should I stay and sit the next course? Should I go to Igatpuri?'

Goenka became serious, 'I cannot tell what you should or shouldn't do. That is not my place. You have to make up your own mind. But you have had a very strong experience. It may be better for you to take a little time to sort out what has happened to you. Then if you wish you could come to Igatpuri.'

Bombay was hot and crowded. It felt different from the northern cities, it felt desperate. I went back to the Japanese temple, and was turned away again. I stood on the temple steps with no idea of what to do or where to go. I had come a full circle. Somewhere in the previous days I had lost momentum, I had not made up my mind if I wanted to go to Igatpuri. Deep down I was afraid of what I might find. After the course in Jaipur I had my hair cut off, down to my scalp, then I shaved off my beard. I didn't want to look like anything. At the hotel I telephoned the youth hostel to see if Palinko and Dieter were there, but they both gone to Delhi. On my way to the railway station in Jaipur, by chance and quite improbably considering the size of the city, I met Jess and Helen. They had come to sit their first meditation course with Goenka. With the end of the cool hippie traveller, the barriers between us had gone, the love was there again.

In Delhi I picked up my luggage and booked a sleeper to Bombay, then I caught a bus out to Palinko's flat. Dieter was staying with him.

'Why did you stop eating?' I asked Palinko again.

'I had such strong memories from my childhood,' he told me, 'they became hallucinations. It was hard to tell what was memory and what was hallucination. I began to believe I had a sickness that I would give to others through the cups and plates, so I stopped drinking and eating. After that I completely lost touch with reality. . . .'

'What about Goenka?' I asked, 'did he know what was going on with you?'

'Oh yes,' said Palinko with confidence, 'Goenkaji was with me all the time...'

I wasn't so sure, but now I wanted Goenka to be enlightened, infallible.

'Will you sit another course?' I asked him.

'I don't know yet. It is too soon, but I am glad I did the course.'

Dieter, as ever, was completely free of doubt. He was just happy to see us both believers on the true path to enlightenment.

Bombay was dark by the time I had made my way from the Japanese temple to Collaba, an area of cheap hotels by the sea front. I went from one sleazy hotel to the next, but they were either full or too expensive. My bags cut into my shoulders and sweat dribbled down my back. Finally I found a greasy room I could just afford. After taking a shower I went for a walk along the sea front in the hot evening air. The pavement was littered with sleeping children, huddled together in filthy ragged heaps, with nothing between them and the pavement. I felt depressed and lonely. I did not want to be part of this cruelty. That night I slept feverishly and woke from a dream with a cry.

In the morning I checked out of the hotel and took my bag to the Victoria terminus station left luggage desk. I wanted to find a better place to stay, but I wanted to be able to move easily, without breaking into a sweat. I walked back down to the sea front and came to the Prince of Wales Museum. Outside a young Indian man, in smart casual clothes, struck up a conversation with me. We chatted for a while, and he told me of the terrible corruption in India.

'When I go for a job in a government position I have to pay five or six thousand rupees,' he told me, 'but even then there is no guarantee of a position.'

'That's terrible,' I said, genuinely shocked.

'I came to Bombay because I am thinking I have work in Saudi Arabia. I am paying six thousand rupees to an agent for a job there,' he sighed looking at his tea cup, 'it was a trick; now I have no job and also I am not able to be going home.'

'How much would you need to get home?' I asked. He had been so friendly and had not even asked me for money.

'Well,' he said forlornly, 'I am needing one hundred rupees to buy a ticket.'

'I can give you a hundred rupees,' I said rashly.

'No!' he said with surprise, 'but that is wonderful. You are sure?'

'Yes,' I said, aware that it could all be a set up, but wanting to believe him, wanting to feel I was doing something to help someone, 'Yes,' I said, 'I am sure.'

Back out on the street I wandered along the pavements in front of expensive down town shop fronts. Hustlers appeared from the shadows offering to change money or supply drugs.

'Hey missster, you want change money....'

'Hello friend, change money....'

'Hey brother, you like good heroin....'

'Hey man, you want fuck, you want change money....'

I walked on ignoring them all. Then, as I was browsing in the window of an Arts and Crafts Emporium, a slick, plump and well dressed man came up to me.

'Hi,' he said removing his sun glasses, 'I wonder if you could help me out?'

His accent was smooth, the English casually fluent.

'How can I help you?' I asked surprised.

'Well, I own an emporium down on the sea front. The Chandra Emporium. Do you know it?' he enquired amiably.

'Well, no,' I said, 'I don't know it.'

'Never mind,' he said, brushing this aside, 'if you help me we can go there. We have a lot of very beautiful craft items at the best prices,' he went on, 'My problem is this. I get paid a lot of cash dollars which I want to take out of the country to my shop in London. If I pay them through the bank I have to pay fifty percent in tax to the government. If I have travellers cheques I can take them out without a problem, but if I buy them as an Indian I also have to pay tax. So you can help me by buying travellers cheques for me. If you buy me a thousand dollars of cheques I'll pay you two hundred dollars.'

'I buy the cheques with your money,' I asked dubiously, 'and you pay me to do it?'

'Yes,' he said with assurance, 'I will give you a thousand dollars cash and you buy the cheques. As a foreigner you do not get taxed.'

'Look,' he said suddenly, checking his watch, 'in half an hour I'm meeting an American fellow, he bought some for me yesterday. If you want to earn a little extra cash, then come to that cafe over there in half an hour. His name is Rick,' he looked seriously into my eyes, 'I picked you because I felt I could trust you. I've already had a French guy walk off with my money. Can I trust you?'

'I wouldn't take your money,' I said sincerely, 'you can trust me.'

'Okay,' he said looking at me for a while, 'I think I can.' He held out his hand, 'my name is Patel, what's yours?'

'Ken .'

'Okay Ken ,' he said, and we shook hands.

I was amazed. One minute I give someone a hundred rupees and the next I am offered two hundred dollars. Karma works I thought. Things were looking up.

I went to the cafe and waited. After twenty minutes Patel arrived and sat with me, then Rick turned up. He sat down with us.

'Hi man, you going to do some cheques with Patel?' asked Rick in a friendly way.

'Is it okay?' I asked, 'does it work?'

'Well man,' said Rick, 'I did a thousand yesterday and he paid me.'

Patel smiled at me reassuringly. I chatted with Rick about India. He said he had arrived three weeks earlier. Although his clothes were clean I noticed his trainers were incredibly dirty and broken. Inside his ear there was a black crust where the soap had not reached. I noted these things, but as we chatted easily together I felt already he was my friend, and why would my friend, a fellow traveller, lie to me?

Patel got up saying he would get a taxi. A few moments later he was back bustling in, the business man with no time to waste.

'Okay boys, are you ready? Then let's go.'

We all got into the taxi.

'First we will go to my shop to collect the cash,' said Patel.

We drove down the back streets towards the sea front.

Patel turned to me and said suddenly, 'I will need to have your traveller cheques as a security when I give you the cash dollars. Okay?'

This was new, I was flustered. I looked at Rick.

'It's okay, I gave him mine yesterday,' he said reassuringly.

'How much do you have?' asked Patel.

'Well,' I told him reluctantly,' I've got a hundred and forty pounds.'

I had collected this in Delhi, sent out by my father.

Patel looked surprised, even shocked. 'Is that all? Only a hundred and forty pounds? Well,' he said, sounding almost angry, 'I guess I'll just have to trust you.'

The taxi suddenly pulled in behind one of the main city bank buildings and Patel got out.

'Why have we stopped here?' I asked as Rick got out too, things were happening too quickly.

'Give me your cheques,' Patel demanded.

'Why now?' I asked, getting suddenly nervous.

'Look,' said Patel, agitated, 'my brother works here at the bank. I want him to check that your cheques are not stolen,' he stared at me, 'look friend I'm going to trust you with a thousand dollars of my money. So give them to me. I don't have all day.'

He seemed very agitated and aggressive. Rick took out a thick book of American Express traveller cheques.

'Two thousand bucks,' said Rick handing them to Patel, 'take care of them.'

Patel quickly flipped through them, then turned to me, his hand out. Uneasily I took out my meagre one hundred and forty pounds traveller cheques and handed them over. Patel took them and set off immediately towards the back of the bank and disappeared. As we waited I talked to Rick about the suffering and corruption that is so evident in Bombay. He agreed it was indeed dreadful. The minutes passed. After ten minutes I was getting worried.

'You don't think he's tricked us do you?' I asked Rick.

'Well it worked yesterday,' Rick said, but with a hint of doubt in his voice.

Another ten minutes passed, and by now Rick and I were pacing up and down. After half an hour it was obvious Patel was not coming back.

'We must stop our cheques as soon as possible,' I cried illogically, believing that if Patel cashed them they would be lost for ever.

'You are right!' said Rick, 'which bank are your cheques with?'

'Grindlay's,' I said. It was an Indian bank.

'Mine are with American Express,' he said, 'look man, I'm sorry about this. It was okay yesterday.'

We set off running in different directions, as Rick disappeared around the corner at the end of the street the bubble burst. I turned to run after him but hesitated. It was all so dreadfully obvious; I had been a victim, not only of Patel and Rick, but of myself. I was a believer.

The next morning I moved from my sleazy hotel to the Salvation Army around the corner. A lot of young travellers stayed there. The large airy dormitories had white painted, metal frame beds, the quiet lounge and dining area were spacious with old easy chairs and magazines. It was staffed by gentle Indians in white shirts and trousers, with names like Christopher, Peter and John. It had the feel of a nineteen thirties sanatorium. At the check-in there was a notice warning guests of con men who offered money to buy traveller cheques. One evening, a few days later, in a large coffee house I saw

Rick. His head was lolling into a plate of half eaten food. He was in a heroin induced oblivion. As I stood by him, waiting to see if he would look up and recognise me, one of the waiters sauntered over and pulled a lighter from his pocket. With an expression of undisguised contempt he held it alight below Rick's unresponsive face.

'Don't,' I said, pulling the waiter's arm away, 'leave him alone.'

I was no longer sure that I even wanted to stay in India. My life there seemed utterly meaningless. My life seemed built on sand, on fantasies that had no value. I began to think about returning west and finding some voluntary work. At least then, I reasoned, I would be contributing something useful to mankind. But the idea of stepping off the plane at Heathrow filled me with a sinking sadness. I didn't want to go back and I didn't want to be where I was. In the lounge area of the Salvation Army I met John. He had recently spent six months at the Goenka centre in Igatpuri.

'I am going to visit Nisagadatta,' John told me one morning, 'do you know about him?'

I remembered the name. Sally at Balcony House had been reading a big book of his dialogues, and Barbara had mentioned him in her letter about where to go and who to see in India.

'I've heard about him,' I said.

'Why don't you come with me to see him? I'm going over this afternoon. I was meant to be going every day this week but I haven't managed to get it together.'

That afternoon I travelled across Bombay with John on a series of crowded buses. We ended up down a ramshackle street in a poor quarter of the city. From a court yard we entered an old house through a low door with a sagging lintel, and climbed an ancient and rickety stairway. The stairs ended in a second story room. The room was already quite full with around twenty people, sitting cross legged on old rugs on the floor. They were mostly Indian, but also half a dozen other westerners. We found a space to sit at the back. A few people spoke quietly, and there was a hush of expectancy in the room.

Nisagadatta was a small, thin old man with a face worn by life. He wore simple, cotton clothes and, without ceremony, sat on the flat padded area at the front and cast his gaze around the room. He was silent for a few moments then, through his translator, who sat at his side, he began to question the newcomers. Sitting near me on one side was a typical Rajneesh Sanyasin. He had long hair, beard and wore burgundy clothes. Around his neck on a string of beads hung the small round photo of Bhagwan.

Nisargadatta nodded at him.

'Why have you come here? You have a Guru,' he demanded bluntly.

'I wish to meet other teachers,' replied the sanyasin anxiously.

'Rajneesh is a big man. He is your Guru. Go to him,' Nisagadatta replied almost crossly.

'But my Guru says I should try to visit all the great masters,' complained the sanyasin.

'No,' said Nisagadatta, 'you have a Guru. You can go. Now.'

The embarrassed Sanyasin got up, stepped between the seated figures and disappeared down the stairs. Nisagadatta then turned his attention to me.

'Why have you come here,' he demanded.

'I came with my friend,' I said nervously gesturing to John, but as this sounded rather weak I added, 'I have been meditating with Goenka.'

Nisagadatta looked at me for a few seconds, sniffed dismissively and turned his attention on John.

'You came here at the beginning of the week. I said you should come every day for five days. You have not come back until now.'

'I had things I needed to do,' said John weakly.

'You are not serious enough. You can go too,' said Nisagadatta.

'But..' said John.

Nisagadatta interrupted him. 'If you are serious, then when you say you will do something, you do it! Now go.'

As John disappeared down the stairs I hoped I would be able to find my way back alone. Nisagadatta questioned a few other visitors, and then he settled down, and was open to questions.

'I am a Frenchman,' said a man at the front, 'I have been practising meditation for ten years.'

'And after ten years,' asked Nisagadatta, 'are you any nearer your goal?'

'Maybe a little nearer,' said the man, 'but it is hard work.'

'The Self is near and the way is easy,' replied Nisagadatta, 'all you need doing is doing nothing.'

'But it is not easy,' said the Frenchman, 'it is difficult.'

'You only have to Be. The doing happens. Just be watchful,' said Nisagadatta, 'where is the difficulty in remembering that you are? You are all the time.'

'But my thoughts, endlessly come and go, their chatter distracts me.'

'Watch your thoughts as you watch the street traffic,' replied Nisagadatta, 'do not struggle with your memories and thoughts, try to include them in your field of attention, together with more important questions, like, Who am I? How did I happen to be born? What is real and what is momentary?' he went on, 'take full advantage of the fact that to experience you must be. You need not stop thinking. Don't hold on, that is all. The world is made of rings. The hooks are all yours. Make straight your hooks and nothing can hold you. Be effortless, stop your routine of acquisitiveness, your habit of looking for results and the freedom of the universe is yours.'

At the end of the meeting, as Nisagadatta began to descend the stairs, he stopped, looked at me and spoke gruffly. After he had gone I found the translator.

'What did he say to me?' I asked.

The translator replied simply.

'He said you are lost in yourself.'

A few days later I met a young Australian called Duncan. He knew of an Australian couple who had arrived in Bombay harbour with a Malaysian junk. They were sailing to Europe and were looking for paying passengers who knew about boats. He was thinking of going with them, and they were looking for one more person. I wondered if I was seeing a way to make the transition from east to west. Rather than just get on a plane and step off twelve hours later, the boat journey would give me time to make the transition. By the end of the next day I had visited the boat, met the owners and the other passengers. The junk was rough, it had no electrical navigational aids, they didn't even have a two-way radio. But they had come all the way from Australia, and were confident about the rest of the journey. I was drawn by the adventure of it, and was given a couple of days to make up my mind. Back on dry land I went to the main post office and rang home. It was a bad line, but I told my mother I was coming home on a Malaysian Junk. Could they send me the money for the passage?

My mother was anxious, 'Ken, is it safe?' she asked.

'Of course it's safe,' I shouted through the crackle.

A new plan formed in my mind, pushing back the fears. I would return to England and take up a meaningful, caring job. I saw myself sitting in meditation each morning and evening, living a life of ordered peace and calm.

That evening someone passed me a chillum and as the hashish hit my brain the fantasies began to break up, the ordered picture sank into a sea of chaotic thoughts and fears. I realised that the caring job was an escape, another fantasy; my motivation was my own well being, not the well being of others. I was like a monkey in a cage running from one part to the next, trying to find the section containing happiness. Left with my confusion as the only truth I knew, I began to remember how I had set off with the intention of going to Igatpuri. Stripped now of hope, of dreams and plans, I remembered the silence, I remembered the suffering I had touched, the pain of it and the beauty of it. I knew then that I had to go on.

The next morning in a state of emotional exhaustion, I went to the bus station to get the bus to Igatpuri. It was hot and chaotic with buses coming and going, and crowds pushing and shoving. I could not work out which bus I should be taking. In the end, out of desperation, I boarded the bus I hoped was going to Igatpuri. It pulled out before I was even seated. Frantically I asked the other passengers if I was on the Igatpuri bus but I received only blank stares. I started shouting in panic. A loud male voice, full of crushing authority, bellowed at me from the back of the bus.

'Sit down and shut up! You are not in Europe now!'

I turned to see a tall Indian, in his thirties. He wore a blazer and flannels. He was a captain of cricket, drawn up in self importance, glowering at me.

'Sit down!' he ordered again.

So I dropped into an empty seat, bewildered, humiliated and exhausted. The bus drove through the chaotic streets taking me I knew not where. I leant my head on my arms and fought back tears.

Chapter 7

The next weeks at Dharmagiri I worked hard. No more spacing out, no more making dreams. I worked as Goenka said I would have to work. I came back again and again to the breath and sensation. I found pain which seemed to tear me apart from the inside. I sat, drenched in sweat, trying to bore my consciousness beyond any boundary. For the first few days I was so exhausted at the end of each session I fell onto my bed and slept. Along with the pain in my body was the fear in my mind. There was a tremendous resistance to change, a deep fear of the unknown, of loneliness, of not being. It felt as if I were spending the day at a cliff edge in a strong wind. In one way it felt that if I could jump I would be free, but somehow I could not reach the place to let go through striving and effort. I 'gave service' during the next ten day course, serving food, doing work around the centre and only sitting three hours a day. Then I sat for a three-day course. After this I decided I'd done enough meditation. There was a limit to how long I wanted to stay at Dharmagiri.

The night before I planned to leave I had a dream. In the dream I had climbed a staircase that spiralled up the inside of a wide shaft. I had nearly reached the top when the stairs narrowed and became little more than odd footholds. It was dangerous, I could easily have fallen. Odd little, alien beings appeared in front of and behind me urging me on and helping me. With their help I made it to the top. When I awoke I decided I should stay on and negotiate the difficulties ahead. I had not quite reached the top of the tower. When I began sitting again a great storm hit me. I raged, postulated, lusted and craved through a wild roller coaster of mind states. In the end

I had to come back to the quiet cell and the sensations, and face the fact that my suffering was all self created.

I wanted very much to go to Goenka and tell him about my journey; he was now such a big part of my life. He was my teacher. On the last night of the course, as I slept, I heard a voice calling me, 'come Kenneth, come...' It was Goenka's voice. I found myself drawn down from a white, weightless world into the room where Goenka met with students. He sat with his wife by his side and motioned for me to sit in front of him. I felt a tremendous sense of being loved.

'Now,' he said gently, 'tell me about yourself.'

So I did. How I was on a journey trying to understand my life, how I had come to India and how I wanted to know what it meant to love without fear. As I finished speaking I heard a bell ring, a long clear tone, Goenka smiled, it was the Burmese gong used at the centre. I listened to the notes, and as I listened I realised I was in bed and it was time to get up.

During the next course Laurie arrived. He was allocated the other place in my two person meditation cell. So Laurie and I sat together for twelve hours a day for ten days in a small dark room observing our own inner worlds. By the end of this course I knew, for the moment, I had done enough. Laurie and I decided to travel on together. He was in a mess, having plumbed some hidden and painful depth, where as I, in contrast, felt calm and rather spiritual. I had gone through something, I had found an inner quiet and I was feeling good.

Perhaps because we had shared a meditation cell, Laurie and I seemed to share the same thoughts, the same irritations, dipping in and out of each others consciousness. We set off together travelling by train to Poona, home of the most famous Guru of them all, Bhagwan shri Rajneesh. On the train I held forth about being in a meditative state.

'It is being able to observe mind states as passing and impermanent,' I told Laurie, 'then you do not suffer, but remain detached.'

'Meditation is not about reaching some stupid, peaceful state where you can feel detached.' Laurie said angrily.

'It's not a stupid state,' I returned defensively, 'I'm just being aware of impermanence.'

'Yes,' replied Laurie, 'but it's only because you feel good. You could just as easily feel completely shitty and observe impermanence.'

He looked angrily at me.

'Well,' I said sanctimoniously, 'I'm not indulging.'

'Oh fuck you,' said Laurie, looking out of the window.

At a small station where we had to change trains our anger reached a point of near hatred.

'I can walk away from this,' I thought, 'I don't have to stay.'

And I knew Laurie was thinking the same.

We travelled the rest of the way to Poona in silence, and by the time we arrived Laurie was in good spirits, but I was feeling as if the carpet had been pulled from under my feet. The great rush of anger I had felt had completely ruined the detached and happy state in which I had left Dharmagiri. Laurie was quick to see the inconsistencies in Goenka's discourses.

'Just to be aware of what ever sensation you experience is fine,' said Laurie, 'but Goenkaji says - after some time you will feel subtle sensations - so all sensations are not equal. The subtle sensations are more important than the gross stuff, by implication.'

'And,' I continued getting his point, 'there can be no gradual path to awakening. It's a pathless land.'

This was the teaching of J. Krishnamurti. I always carried one of his books. In his teachings I found a raw truth. He often talked about meditation, but he constantly said there could be no technique to see the truth. Intriguingly, Krishnamurti was adamant that any attempt to practise meditation was not meditation at all. Krishnamurti spoke straight to my heart, his teachings demanded I understand, now.

The streets of Poona were unusually clean, and the town looked prosperous. A suitable home for Rajneesh, Guru of the libido, owner of a dozen Rolls Royces. His ashram, with a sign demanding: 'Shoes and minds to be left at the door,' was like a tropical health spa. The kitchens were a spectacle of spotless, stainless steel. German cooks prepared health food, which was sold by pretty French girls from immaculate, glass topped display cabinets at European prices. After India it was oddly unfamiliar, and I found I preferred the grubby chai shops, germs and all, to the imperialistic slickness of the ashram. The ashram did not feel Indian, it was like an ex-patriot spiritual ghetto with an armed guard at the gates. There was a price tag on every item and every teaching. It was quite a shock after the austerity and donations only generosity of Dharmagiri.

The Rajneesh Sanyasins wore the traditional saffron colours of renunciation in every possible hue, and in a variety of fashions. It seemed to me they were taking an ancient tradition and making a mockery of it, adopting it as the uniform of their sexy club. The only things they renounced, as far as I could see, were their inhibitions, and large amounts of cash into the Ashram coffers.

I went along for a taped, evening discourse. The hall was full of languid Sanyasins caressing, stroking and lolling against each other. I sat alone, half envying them their freedom, half despising them their gullibility. The theme of the evening talk was, to my surprise, Krishnamurti. Krishnamurti was openly hostile to all Gurus who asked for followers, and although he never named names, he was particularly irritated by Rajneesh. Krishnamurti, perhaps like Nisargadatta, had banned

Rajneesh Sanyasins from his talks.

'The speaker,' said Krishnamurti, 'abhors the worship of a personality.'

Rajneesh spent the entire talk trying to discredit Krishnamurti by implying his prejudice was just sexual hang-ups.

'AH can accept the teaching of Krishnamurti,' said Rajneesh in triumph, 'but HE cannot accept MAH teaching!'

The next evening, finding myself without cigarettes in a cafe, I asked a Sanyasin nearby if he could spare one. He took one out then threw it on the floor.

'There it is if you want it,' he said.

Laurie and I decided it was time to move on.

The next morning we went to a cycle shop in the town and bought a couple of Indian bicycles. We strapped our back packs onto the luggage racks and, feeling like an Asian version of Peter Fonda and Dennis Hopper, peddled off south towards Goa. We slept in villages and by the road. At one small town on the way, as I walked through the bazaar, dressed in a turban and dirty white cotton clothes, a shop keeper asked me if I was from Kashmir.

'Na Baba,' I said, 'Englisthan.'

I walked on savouring the happiness of being mistaken for an Indian in India. A week later we turned off the hot plains and, screaming with delight, tore down through the forested ghats onto the steamy coastal heat of Goa below. We rented a room for a week or so and rested.

We sold our bikes and took the bus two hundred miles inland to Hampi, an ancient city of ruined temples. We lived among the ruins, bathing in the cool waters of the fast flowing river. We ate at the village chai shops and slept in the empty temple buildings. For the first time in my life I meditated every day. I believed I had found what I was looking for. I was a meditator. I felt I had found security within the insecure.

I visited the ancient Shiva temple, which was still in use. It was built for a city that had long gone, and the blackened temple buildings rose, as strange as science fiction, above the few mud houses outside its gates. I sat in a corridor of the temple surrounded by carved stone pillars. Around me stone deities rested silently in barred caverns. In the half light of the inner sanctum a black, stone bull stared at a massive lingam. Women came and touched their heads on the lingam, and drank a little of the water that trickled down its sides. The air was thick with incense, spirits and magic. Power vibrated through the stone bulk of the place. The Priests, in white dhotis and sacred threads, their bodies dark and lithe, scurried from place to place with the ingredients of their rituals. They were like the engineers running a spiritual power station. They lubricated and fed, channelling Shiva's forces of fertility, liberation, confusion and destruction.

Laurie wanted to go back to Igatpuri. I decided to go to Bodhgaya, the site of the Buddha's enlightenment. We parted at the bus station, both launching off into the unknown, with a minimum of fuss. I took a local bus to the nearest main line station, not really knowing where I was going. On the map, Bodhgaya was six hundred miles to the north, and I was in India's heartlands with no tourists or tourist quotas. I ended up on the floor of a train, spread out on my cotton blanket. Ten hours rumbling through the Indian night, watched by crowded, dark eyes.

Alone again my mind wandered into fantasy. I had sharp pains in my side and I wondered about my liver, whether it was damaged beyond repair by hepatitis. I remembered the bag of unwashed grapes I had eaten at the station, fearful of sickness, but greedy for the sweet taste. I tried to sleep but my mind was too full, too wired up. I felt so apart, so disconnected from all the normal lives around me, yet at the same time connected to something deeper, to the part of India that allowed men and women to smear their bodies with ash and go forth. A land where God was intertwined in every aspect of life. I answered the questions of people I could never know, and who would never know me. From which country are you coming? What is your business? Are you married? They wanted to know about tribe, money and sex. I was free of cultural limitations, no one expected me to behave in any particular way. I could reinvent myself moment by moment. I was free to explore the chaotic and painful phenomena called 'me'.

I arrived exhausted in Secunderabad in the early hours of the morning. I found a quiet hall and fell asleep on a bench. When I awoke I got some tea and shared it with a beggar boy. There seemed to be beggars everywhere and a ruined poverty that pervaded everything. I found the next train I had to take and set off again. The journey was punctuated by towns, Chandrapur, Nagpur, Raipur. We rumbled into towns past their sprawling shanty town suburbs, and through the decaying town centres. At one main station I was faced with real poverty. A small boy came shuffling along the floor, ineffectually sweeping up our filth with a rag. He held his hand out for a few paisa, but mostly he received only a rude rebuttal. He was followed by a legless man, then a dwarf and a woman with a dying child. A blind man came through the carriage and began to sing. He sang a lament and his voice was so beautiful, so heart breakingly sad, I almost cried out.

The day turned to night and when the next dawn came we were in Orissa. The dawn sun threw translucent light over the misty paddy fields. The palm trees looked like brush stokes. A group of loud young men in nylon bell bottoms took up the seats around me and began to talk about me, mockingly, laughing loudly. Opposite a thin peasant sat cross legged, his wife asleep leaning against him. On his lap, his four year old daughter rested her head on his shoulder, she looked across at me. We looked for a long time into each others' eyes, and then softly, tenderly, she gave me a smile full of love.

My train was destined for Calcutta, a fact that began to trouble me. I did not want to have to deal with another big Indian city, especially one with Calcutta's reputation. Looking on my map I noticed the train passed close to Puri, on the eastern coast. I knew Puri was famous for the Juggernaut idol, and the enormous medieval cart upon which it was wheeled out once a year. It was a pilgrimage place for devotees of Krishna. I also knew Puri was a seaside town, the Brighton of Calcutta. I wondered if it would be a place to have a couple of days resting, eating good food and hanging out on the beach. When the train stopped in a small town twenty miles inland, I grabbed my bag and, pushing through the crowded aisles, jumped down on to the platform. I walked out through the station building onto a small square, and crossed over to a couple of waiting buses.

'Puri?' I called up to the driver .

'Puri,' he replied, wobbling his head.

An hour later I stood, looking around, feeling lost in the bustle of Puri town square. The streets were packed with stalls, cows, beggars, lorries and over-loaded carts pulled by sweating coolies. There was much jostling, shouting and blowing of horns. No one came up and offered 'cheap hotel'. Wanting to get away from the heat and noise, I decided to go to the beach. Following directions I set off down a narrow road packed with pilgrims. The sides of the road were lined with beggars. There were men sitting in thorn bushes, lepers with no hands, mutants, men with bandages oozing something too red to be real blood. It was a long hot half mile with the stream of pleas from the beggars, and my bag getting steadily heavier. Finally, when I came out onto the beach, my heart sank. It was covered in fishing boats, assorted fishing tackle and was overlooked by a village of poor mud houses. I had expected something a little more developed, like Goa, a place where I could easily find a room and the company of other travellers.

Finding a chai shop I dropped my bag and ordered chai and a cake. It was getting late and I was tired but, without a hotel, I was not quite sure what to do next. Sitting alone at a table near mine, I noticed a young and pretty Indian woman in a sari. She looked the epitome of a young middle-class Indian woman. Unexpectedly she began to talk to me.

'Have you just arrived in Puri?' she asked.

'Yes,' I said, rather thrown by what was happening, 'I've just walked from the bus stand.'

I looked at her and a wave of confused feelings rushed through me. It was more than just the unfamiliarity of being approached by an unchaperoned Indian girl. It was, I realised as I looked into her eyes, that she was exuding a powerful sexuality. I struggled to remain composed.

'I don't usually talk to Westerners,' she said, in a perfect middle class English accent, 'but there was something about you.'

'Oh?' I replied, thinking, can the Buddha be taking pity on me? Are all my sexual fantasies about to be fulfilled?

'What particularly about me?' I asked nervously.

'Something... ' she hesitated, '...something unthreatening,' she smiled shyly.

'Well,' I said, 'I think that's reassuring.'

She laughed and gave me an incredibly sexy smile. Her name was Melissa, she was English and she had been to art school. Her mother was of Indian descent, her father was Anglo Saxon. As we talked I realised her sari was a bit of a charade, that Melissa was not much more Indian than I was. She was serious about avoiding westerners though, and there weren't any others in this rather dead end seaside bit of Puri. After tea Melissa suggested that I take a room at the house where she was staying. So we set off together into the village behind the beach. She led me to a proper three story house standing proudly halfway down a road of mud shacks. I was shown a simple but clean room with a sea view, and fussed over by the old couple who owned the place.

The next day I spent with Melissa. It was like being fifteen again, where, if the connection was right, kissing and groping might be on the agenda as easily as Monopoly or bike rides. The trouble with Melissa was I couldn't quite work out our connection. All I knew was that I desired her so much I could think of little else. We caused quite a stir when we walked through the town together. I was the ragged hippie, she was a wealthy Indian girl from a good home. Conversation stopped when we walked past, and the yearning of people to know about us was tangible. We chatted amiably, but it was clear that neither of us had much to say of interest to the other. She told me bluntly that she was not interested in sex at all. At first I was shocked, but then I looked at her and she was so incredibly sexy, I just knew it couldn't be true.

That evening back at our house Mataji, the old mother, cooked for us. We sat cross-legged and ate from big stainless steel plates. Afterwards we took a walk along the sea front. I jogged along next to Melissa, she always strode along as if slightly late. At a chai shop we sat under the bright, white neon lights next to mounds of sticky pastries and drank a glass of hot sweet chai. Then we walked together onto the moon-lit beach. Melissa chattered endlessly on until I could hardly bear it. I wanted to touch her, to feel her warmth. I came close and put my arm around her. She pulled away from me.

'I need my space,' she said, in a voice suddenly tense with fear.

I remained silent, feeling a mixture of contrition and rejection. We walked on in silence, then sat down, not too close, and stared out towards the dark ocean. I hugged my knees against the cool, on-shore breeze.

Melissa began to tell me about her sex life. It had been one long catalogue of sexual encounters. She seemed to have been making love, having sex, copulating and fucking non stop since she was fourteen.

'All the boys wanted to fuck me,' she told me, 'I tried it with some of them, I felt as if I ought to.' She'd been raped, she'd been abused, she'd been seduced. She told me about one incident after the other until her words rang in my head.

'I fucked some of them because I felt I ought to, but others I fucked because I liked them.'

Screwing, being fucked, and fucking, and fucking and fucking. That word, so awful, sounded so neat in her middle-class, well spoken accent. I couldn't bear it because that was what I wanted from her too. I envied her abusers, her lovers, her seducers. Why did I have to be her confessor? Why did she have to trust me? What had I done to deserve this? As Melissa talked on and on I began to sing. I sang 'Hari Krishna, Hari Rama,' the old Krishna devotees song. Jess and I used to sing it for fun, enjoying the easy harmonies. I started quietly while she continued speaking, but I began to sing louder and louder until I was singing at the top of my voice. I was singing the song to Krishna, the God of sensuality, of sex, of love. I sang to blow away her pain, to transcend the worldly madness of her confusion and my craving. I stopped singing suddenly, embarrassed, plunging us into silence. She got up, said she was going to bed and walked off across the sand. I was left feeling stupid, alone, transparent like a ghost.

The next morning I tried to meditate. The daily meditation sessions I had with Laurie after Igatpuri had somehow been lost on the train journey. I took up the cross legged posture and began to observe my breath, but set against the intensity of my desire it seemed a hopeless act, as futile as a soldier crossing himself before going into battle. I meditated for twenty minutes, and for nineteen of them thought only of Melissa. When we met later, she did not mention the night before. The afternoon passed by and, as before, Melissa talked incessantly, never pausing to ask me anything. She continued describing her past sex life. I continued to listen as her confidant, being friendly, and secretly hoping my turn would come. I felt as if I had been drawn off the train by Melissa's magic and was now stuck, not knowing how to undo the spell, a prisoner of my own desire.

The next evening after another late chai we walked again down across the sand towards the sea. We were surrounded by the unearthly glow of the full moon.

'I'm afraid,' Melissa said suddenly, 'I want to go back.'

'There's no need to be afraid,' I said, 'sit down, look at the sea, it's beautiful.'

We sat on the sand and stared out. The moon glittered on the black water, the waves broke like exploding effervescent snakes.

'I want to touch you,' I said, 'just to give you a hug.'

'Is that all you want?' she asked, accusingly.

'No,' I confessed, 'I do want more than that.'

I put my arm out to her.

'Don't do this to me,' she said angrily, pulling away, 'why do you keep doing that?'

'I'm sorry,' I told her, 'I just find you very attractive.'

'That,' she replied coldly, 'is what all the others said.'

Her words burst the bubble, the spell was broken. My desire for Melissa drained out of me like water from a sink. Without the desire I felt empty, back with the painful truth. I was alone.

The next day Melissa came with me to Puri branch line station. We were uncomfortably intimate with one another, like a brother and sister who did not get on. There was no exchange of addresses, no 'maybe see you in....' I waved from the window as the train pulled out. She stood alone on the platform in her red sari, waving back.

Fifteen hours later I arrived in Gaya. I took a motor rickshaw from the station to the village of Bodhgaya. The landscape was empty and dry. The road ran along the bank of an empty river, so wide the rocky hills on the far bank were just pale blue silhouettes in the cool morning light. At the outskirts of the village the rickshaw stopped by the entrance to a walled compound.

'Burmese Vihara,' said the rickshaw driver.

I entered the compound and stood looking around, my rucksack at my feet. The compound edges were crowded with buildings, some were crude, single story huts, some were two-story houses. There were lots of trees and a flower garden struggling out of the baked ground. An Indian boy, seeing me arrive, ran off and returned a few moments later with the Abbot. He wore the dark saffron robes of the Theravadin tradition and was smoking a cheroot. He looked very laid-back. The vihara was a monastery, a rest house for pilgrims. Since the Burmese government had made travel virtually impossible for the Burmese, the vihara had become the Westerner vihara, an enclave of Buddhists and travellers.

I was given a cell like room, eight foot square, built of crude concrete. It had an iron bed with a mosquito net, a metal door and a small window covered in broken mesh. In the corner there was a rickety table covered in wax dribbles from countless candles. After I had unpacked a few things I set off into the village. I wanted to see the spot where prince Gotama had attained Nirvana and become Gotama the Buddha. As I came close to the village centre I could see a hundred foot stupa towering above the trees. The stupa enclosure was surrounded by wrought iron railings that would not have looked out of place in Kensington Gardens. The enclosure itself was terraced down twenty feet below ground level to the base of the stupa. At one side of the stupa's base there was an ancient and sprawling Bodhi tree. Its horizontal branches had grown so long they had been propped up. A notice explained this tree had been grown from a cutting of the Bodhi tree in Sri Lanka, which had been grown from a cutting off the original tree under which the Buddha had sat. Tibetan pilgrims had festooned it with prayer flags. Some were new and brightly coloured, others were as washed out as old tissue paper. There were so many they looked like refuse left from a passing flood. The gardens were full of small shrines and Buddha statues. I walked down to the main shrine room at the base of the stupa and paid my respects to the Buddha.

I spent the next few days meditating in the gardens surrounding the Stupa. I walked around the walkway that surrounded the Stupa grounds, accompanied by cheerful, ragged Tibetan pilgrims swinging prayer wheels and mumbling mantras. Each evening monks from Sri Lanka chanted for half an hour. Although the tune was different I recognised the Pali words from Goenka's chanting.

'Namo tassa, Bhagavato, Arahato, Sammasam Buddha sa... '

They were taking refuge. Although this was the focal point of one of the world's great religions, the feeling around the Stupa was completely relaxed and unpretentious. There were no areas for the select few, no priests giving orders and getting paid, there was just a friendly assortment of pilgrims hanging out together. I realised, with genuine surprise, that I was one of them.

During the following days I became infected with the energy

of Bodhgaya. I began to consider becoming a Buddhist monk. I wanted to continue with meditation, the Buddha's path, so to become a monk was a logical step. I could see myself in the robes, bare foot, with a begging bowl, walking with downcast eyes, absorbed in mindfulness. It looked good, like a photo in a magazine. But the decision was not easy, I had many doubts. I wondered if I could look at a pretty girl and observe my reactions with detachment. I wondered, more importantly, if I even wanted to. And if I became a monk, should I be a monk alone in India, or go to Burma, or Thailand and live in a monastery?

At Shivanath's I met an American couple who had just completed a three year retreat with Kalu Rimpoche in Darjeeling. Kalu Rimpoche, they told me, was enlightened. We discussed the differences between the southern school of Theravadan Buddhism and the Mahayana Buddhism of Tibet. They warned me off Goenka's interpretation of Vipassana. I told them about how I had seen Goenka as so arrogant and corrupt, and then as full of love and compassion, a mirror for my own negativity.

'But both feelings are you,' said the American man, 'the mistrust and hate and the love and surrender, all you ever see is your own mind.'

Before we parted he gave me Kalu Rimpoche's address and a photo of him. I slotted the idea of visiting Kalu Rimpoche in with my various other plans.

During this time I kept remembering the I Ching I had thrown before coming to India. It had promised great realms after three years, but it had warned of rushing ahead on thin ice. One year had passed since throwing the hexagram. I had two years to go until the thin ice was crossed, until great realms were awarded. Two years to blow it.

Ling Rimpoche, who had lived just around the hill from Balcony house, was visiting Bodhgaya. I decided to visit him and ask his advice about becoming a monk. At the Tibetan temple I was shown into a light and airy room, and directed to where Ling Rimpoche sat on a low podium. I sat cross legged on the floor in front of him. He beamed down at me and filled me with joy.

'I would like to take robes as a monk, but I don't know if it's the right time, or even the right thing for me. What should I do?' I felt foolish, knowing he could not possibly advise me.

He looked at me for a while, then said, 'if you do what you want to do, you will do well.'

I tried to make a decision, but one way or the other, I was troubled by doubts. The days went by in an anxious dither. I had considered going back to England, going to Burma to be a monk, staying in India as a monk, going to Kalu Rimpoche, going to McLeod Ganj, but I only went in circles. I discussed my plans with various acquaintances around the village and in the vihara. I found everyone was ending up with different versions of my future, depending on where I was at the moment they met me.

Then I received a letter from Laurie, who had been sitting at Dharmagiri and he sounded reassuringly confused.

'....I can't sit still for more than ten minutes, very agitated, and I only want to get away from here, so suppose I must stay. Write for yourself 25 pages of my future plans. You won't be far wrong.'

I went and talked with an American Theravadan monk staying at the Vihara. He had been in robes for twenty years. He had lived in monasteries in south east Asia, and travelled round India living by begging in the traditional way.

'If you take robes and stay in India,' he told me, 'you will be left pretty much to your own devices. The main thing as a monk is to keep the vows and rules. That's what it means to be a monk. You can do pretty much what you like, as long as you keep to the rules.' He laughed, 'there's quite a lot of them.'

His unpretentiousness made me realise that putting on orange robes would not change the contents of my head, I would still be the same person, with all the same stuff going on. I knew then I was nowhere near ready to be able live unsupported in India as a Buddhist monk, and I knew too that I did not want to go off to a monastery in Burma or Thailand. So I began to consider returning to the West. Perhaps the time had come to remove myself from all these places. McLeod, Bodhgaya, Puri, Hampi, and all the crazy energy of India. Perhaps it was time to see if what I felt and believed could survive western reality.

Released from indecision I relaxed into Bodhgaya. It was March and the weather had become hotter. Shivanath, the owner of the village chai shop, had got to know me and greeted me, as did the various resident leprous beggars. I knew my way around, and felt the same sense of being at home as I had in Mcleod. At the Mahabodhi society library I read books on Buddhism. I walked around the Stupa, meditated in the grounds and hung out, chatting with other western Buddhists from various traditions. In my room at the Vihara I made an altar with a tiny, but beautiful, brass Tibetan Buddha. Behind it I had a photo of Goenka, and each day I sat, one hour in the morning and one hour in the evening.

Life at the Vihara was punctuated by small dramas and one tragedy. A young Austrian, only nineteen years old, died from a heroin overdose. He had been sleeping in the Vihara hall, home to a big, rather dusty, Burmese Buddha statue. He had been found unconscious, having inhaled his own vomit, and died on the way to hospital. The American monk told me he had had several meetings with him.

'It was sad,' the American said, 'he kept telling me he had been a bad son, and he wanted to make a better life for himself. I gave him a book of the Buddha's sayings,' he paused,

'when they found him, he had the book in one hand and a nee-
dle in the other.'

I thought that there were a lot worse ways to die if you were
a junkie in India. He had turned up, confessed his sins to a
monk, and died reading the Buddha's' teachings. Everyone
agreed he must have been a Buddhist in a previous life.

I met Martin, a rather ragged Australian, who had just
arrived from the ashram of Rajananda in Bihar. He was waiting for money to arrive from Australia. Rajananda was the
Guru of the Marsh Mountain ashram in Australia where I had
stayed. Martin had become a Swami, under the dubious guidance of Bhaktiananda. After several years of being a Swami in
Australia he had asked if he could visit the ashram in India. To
his surprise he was told that in order to go he would need five
thousand dollars. This was shocking news. He was a Swami, a
renunciate, he didn't have money, certainly not five thousand
dollars. But those were the terms. So in the 'he-must-have-
needed-it' school of thought, he disrobed and spent a lonely,
twelve months working in a factory. He saved the money, re-
took his robes and flew to India. In Calcutta he caught dysentery. He arrived at the Rajananda ashram and collapsed,
spending the next week half conscious. To his surprise the
ashram seemed less concerned with his health than in getting
him to sign his travellers cheques, and formally donate them to
the ashram. He lay on a mattress recovering for two weeks and
watched the goings on at the ashram. He didn't like what he
saw. When he recovered sufficiently he told the ashram authorities he wished to leave. This news did not bother them in the
least, but they would not return his money. He had walked to
Bodhgaya as a Swami, living by begging.

'What is it like to live by begging?' I asked, 'I had wondered
about living like that.'

'Forget it,' Martin laughed, 'it was awful. The food is shit, you get loads of hassle, and there is nowhere to sleep,' he looked at me, 'believe me, you wouldn't last a fortnight. I only did it was because I had to get away from the ashram.'

I had made up my mind to go back to England. I intended to book my flight in Delhi and then spend the remaining time in McLeod. One morning I said good-bye to my various friends and acquaintances and set off back to Gaya station. In Delhi I went back to the Anand Hotel where Laurie and I had stayed six months earlier. I got a room and flopped onto the clean white sheets. An hour later I was woken by loud knocking on the door. Laurie burst into the room.

'But how did you know I was here?' I asked.

'I didn't,' said Laurie, smiling in disbelief, 'as I filled in the Hotel register I looked at the name above mine and it was yours!'

We went for tea together and I told Laurie that I was going to leave India. He had been thinking about doing the same. The next day we went to the Thai airways office and booked seats on a flight to London. Outside the office we split up, each of us having different tasks to fulfil. I went to the bazaar in old Delhi to look for gifts for my family. On a busy street an old man with black and intense eyes came tugging at my sleeve.

'Sahib! Sahib! I tell your fortune.'

'No, no. Go away,' I said, but he was insistent. In the end I turned to him, in a challenge just to get rid of him.

'Go on then, tell me something, prove you are for real.'

He looked at me intently, his milky eyes strangely unseeing.

'You stay a long time in India, but you go back your country soon,' he told me, 'First you go mountains, then you come back Delhi, then go your country.'

My mind went blank. It was too much. I didn't want to hear anymore. Someone else was pulling at my sleeve.

'Hey friend you want change money?'

I pulled away and started walking, and when I turned the old man was across the road about to be swallowed by the crowd. I carried on walking towards the hotel, wishing I had stayed, knowing I should have listened.

Two weeks later I was thundering down the runway in a Thai air Jumbo, it was the cleanest thing I'd seen since arriving in India. It felt as clinical as a deep freeze. As it shuddered and left Indian soil, after fourteen months, I said a silent farewell. The pretty air hostess came by smiling, like a nurse in a hospice.

'We must be mad,' I said to Laurie, who stared at the seat in front.

He was meditating, observing his sensations. I had done it. I was going back. But I did not feel like I was going home.

Chapter 8

ENGLAND 1981

The spare room at the top of my parent's house was simply furnished. On the top of a small bookcase I made an altar with a Buddha statue and a photo of Goenka. This was also my sitting corner where I kept a cushion and the cotton shawl in which I wrapped myself when I sat. Each day, as I had in India, I sat for an hour in the morning and an hour in the evening. After three days the initial interest in my return had passed. After two weeks it was hard to believe I had even been away. The house seemed deeply unhappy, it seeped into me, like a gas. The decision to return to the west had seemed a big step to take in India, but now I was back it was done, India was finished, gone. The decision now was, what was I going to do with the rest of my life? I was twenty four, I had been living out of a back pack for five years. I had talked about finding peace and happiness, but I had neither. It was all just ideas and in reality I was confused, unhappy and lonely. I had my meditation practice, but it did little to answer the more mundane questions like where I was going in my life, or even what to do next. So once again I tried the old Art School plan.

'I'm thinking of applying for a place at Bristol School of Art,' I said to my parents one evening.

'Oh, I do think that is a good idea,' said my mother.

My father carried on reading his book.

'What do you think Michael?' she asked him.

He looked up over his glasses.

'Well, you do have the ability,' he said carefully, 'and I've always thought you should make use of it.'

'That's right,' I said, thinking only in terms of daily survival,

'I think I would like living in Bristol.'

After three weeks I hitch-hiked down to London and met up with Laurie. He was staying with friends in Brixton, where there were the first riots on the streets of London for years. Sirens wailed and helicopters hovered in smoke filled skies. The prediction of immanent cultural and economic collapse by the astrologers in McLeod seemed about to come true.

'Most of my friends seem to be getting married and settling down,' said Laurie, 'there aren't many of us bums left.'

'Well, I'll probably go to art school if I can get in,' I told him, 'and I'm not sure about being a bum anyway. I want to live in one place, be part of a community, be creating something.'

'Only because you think it will make you happy,' said Laurie.

I wanted to shout. 'You are wrong!' But Laurie sounded so sure.

'I just don't know.' I said.

'Well that's okay,' he said with humour, 'not knowing is good for meditation. You can only find answers when you don't know.'

'That's easy for you to say,' I replied.

'No,' he said, 'it's not easy for me. It's just you forget I've done all that. I've got a degree. I've had a career. I had a cottage, a girl friend, regular sex, a vegetable garden. I know it's only because you have never been there that you think it will make you happy. But I know you, what you have done. That just isn't going to be your way.'

'Well, maybe it won't make me happy,' I replied, 'but surely it won't make me unhappy.'

'Maybe, maybe not. God, I don't know,' said Laurie wearily, 'maybe it is what you need.'

From London I was planning to go to Splatts House, the U Ba Khin meditation centre in Wiltshire. U Ba Khin had been

Goenka's teacher in Burma. Goenka often talked about his teacher, and, although he had died some years before, he was very much the father of the tradition. I even had his photo on my shrine.

Goenka was one of three U Ba Khin students teaching Vipassana meditation. The other two were Mother Sayama from Burma and John Woodman, an American who lived in England. I had heard about these other teachers while I had been at Igatpuri. Some of the old students at Igatpuri had been to Burma and sat with Mother Sayama. She was reputed to be an Anagami, a never returner, the third of the four stages to Enlightenment. She was talked about with a certain awe.

Splatts House turned out to be a large old farmhouse in a village near Chippenham. I arrived, as I had in India, unannounced. I had been thinking Splatts house would perhaps be a place I could live for a few months, finding some casual work near by. But it only took a few moments to realise it was strictly a meditation centre. There were no private rooms, only dormitory rooms with mattresses on the floor. The day began at four thirty and the house was in silence. If I stayed I would have to either sit a meditation course, or alternatively serve a course by helping run the centre by cooking, cleaning and gardening. I had not sat a meditation course since leaving Igatpuri five months earlier, and so I decided to join the next course. It was to be led by John Woodman and was due to start in a few days.

During the following days at the house I heard how, later in the summer, Mother Sayama was coming back from Burma to stay. There were a lot of Sayama devotees, and the house had been bought primarily as a place where she could live and teach in the west. It was also to be a permanent centre for the other U Ba Khin teachers. Goenka was coming to Splatts house in the summer, as was John Woodman. Three courses, led by the three different teachers, were to run one after the other. It was the first time they had all taught in the same place at the same time, and I planned to sit all three courses. Thirty days of silence and sitting twelve hours a day. I allowed myself to speculate that, perhaps, during this period I was destined for some great insight while sitting with Sayama. She would see my deep spiritual potential, call me to her, touch me on the head. Pow! A tremendous insight, freedom and all my anxiety would be over. I would be happy, at peace.

John Woodman arrived for the course puffing an old pipe and driving a clapped out Ford. He was in his late fifties and overweight, but he had a warm and friendly manner, and greeted me casually with a shake of the hand. He looked more like a scrap metal dealer than a meditation teacher. After the intense Guru relationship I had had with Goenka, it was strange to meet a teacher of the same tradition who was so laid back. I couldn't imagine having his photo on my altar. So under the guidance of John Woodman I began another ten days of sitting. During this retreat my bodily sensations kept dissolving, rather alarmingly, into formlessness. After a few days I lost my fear and could stay with the sense of dissolution. I became suffused by the silence, the sense of calm and love that pervaded the house. I realised then that I could not possibly explain meditation to my parents as I had tried to, since coming back from India. Without knowing this silence any explanation was doomed to be reduced to mere words and ideas. I realised it was not important to convert them, only to love them. Filled with this spiritual calm I saw myself living at home with my parents, bathing them in the silence and happiness I now felt.

When I returned to my parents' house ten days later, the silence and happiness drained away as if I had been unplugged. The sense of inner quiet was replaced by the usual stream of thoughts, anxieties, irritations, plans and fantasies. I watched, fascinated and appalled, at the way my mother and father related to each other. There seemed to be a blanket of suffering that lay over their lives, which I felt so intensely it made me want to scream. I felt it in every turn of phrase, every minor interaction. It filled pages of my diary. I wanted to tear away the shrouds of pain, to shine the light of understanding onto the darkness of their relationship, and by doing so, liberate them. I began to believe I could; that they would be astonished and relieved. I thought it would be like pointing out an unseen thorn. Finally, unable to restrain myself, I confronted my father. He patiently listened to what I had to say. I read him the sections from my diary which analysed his relationship to my mother with the detail of a Victorian anthropologist observing a tribal ritual, seeing everything but knowing nothing. When I finished he was silent for a long time, staring sadly out of the window.

He said quietly, 'don't show that to your mother, will you?'

I had shined my light into his private darkness, and the uselessness of my intrusive words hung silently between us.

I confronted my mother with our past, unable to stop myself.

'Why did you send us away to school?' I asked, going for her weakest point.

'We came to visit you every three weeks,' she defended herself lamely.

'A weekend visit is not a home,' I retorted.

She looked weary, hurt and went upstairs to sew curtains. A few minutes later I followed her.

'I'm sorry,' I said ashamed, 'I don't mean to hurt you.'

'It does hurt,' she said and began to cry.

She rarely cried. I was shocked. I went over and held her. I was appalled and confused by what I had done.

'I would give anything to be able to change it all,' she said.

'No,' I protested, 'it's not like that.'

My father was, rather conveniently, European co-ordinator for an American company that ran hotel barges, and I spent the next two months as a stand-in boatman in France and England. As the weeks passed by I began looking forward to sitting at Splatts house and seeing Goenka again. I had sent off my drawings to Bristol school of art and awaited news. Finally I received a forwarded letter from the college. I opened it sitting on a quay side in a small French town. I had not been accepted. I was surprised to find I felt only relief.

When I arrived back at Splatts House it had been transformed in preparation for Goenka's course. He always attracted large numbers. In the garden there was a marquee large enough to sit several hundred people. The rest of the garden was packed with small tents. In the courtyard a large tent had become a kitchen, with half a dozen people sitting at trestle tables chopping mounds of vegetables. There were port-a-cabin toilets, and a field had been opened as a car park. The sun was shining and the house had a carnival feel to it. There was a lot to do, and, as an old student, I was quickly roped-in to help. When Goenka arrived he was ushered into the house.

'Goenkaji is here!' the excited word went around.

We all transformed into our best meditator behaviour, being mindful, observing our sensations. People were arriving all the time, and there were lots of familiar faces from India and Dharmagiri.

Finally the ten-day course began, silence settled over the house and order settled over the chaos. Things worked, even if it was rather crowded. It was strange to see Goenka teaching in a tent in an English country garden. The sixth day was hot, the tent was silent but for the gentle flap of canvas and the odd cough and shuffle of meditators. Then a loud rasping voice cut through the silence.

'YOU ARE EVIL!'

A man, a participant on the course, was walking between the seated figures towards Goenka. I was transfixed, my heart pounding. No one moved.

Pointing an accusing finger he shouted, 'You are controlling everyone! Brainwasher!'

Goenka, at first as surprised as the rest of us, collected himself and tried to pacify the man.

'Please, there is no need to shout. Please, sit,' he gestured to the space in front of him, 'sit and we can talk.'

Ignoring him, the man turned and spoke desperately to the hall.

'You don't have to stay here! You can leave! You are having your minds taken away from you.'

He turned from side to side, looking imploring at the blank sea of faces. Those running the course were now appearing in their flapping Burmese lungis, looking like security police in drag. They tried to make the intruder leave, but he pulled away.

'Let go of me,' he cried, 'can't you see what's happening? They want to get rid of me because they don't want you to hear what I have to say!'

A few, brave, maverick voices now rose from the back.

'Yeah!' someone cried, 'let him speak!'

'Leave him alone,' another voice joined in, empowered by the first voice of dissent.

And they did, they let go and stepped away. The man stood looking at us and we all looked back. He seemed taken aback at having nothing to push against.

'I'm going!' he shouted suddenly, 'I'm free!'

He pointed to a rather pretty girl sitting near the back. The silence made it easy to have fantasy relationships. Bubbles of illusion that burst with as little consequence as soap bubbles when the silence ended.

'Come with me,' he implored her, 'you don't have to stay here.'

Blushing at the unexpected attention, she said quietly, but firmly, 'I'm okay, I don't want to leave.'

The man then spoke to the crowd again, his voice now desperate, losing it's violence. 'You are fools! Get out while you can.'

The maverick from the crowd called back, 'it's not like that, we're okay, we don't want to leave. No one has to stay.'

'Well, I'm getting out of this shit,' said the man, and walked out, followed by several anxious looking course workers. Goenka was clearly upset by what had happened.

He spoke to us later. 'Please,' he asked, 'do not leave the grounds during the course. As I have explained, this technique of meditation is like doing a deep operation on the mind. It opens up levels in the unconscious and all kind of old Sankaras come to the surface. It is like pus in a wound. You have to remove the pus to allow the wound to heal. Sometimes that is a painful process. It leaves you vulnerable while the operation is going on. Here you are in a protected environment. At the end of the course we will do a Metta meditation on loving kindness which will help to heal any deep wounds that have been opened. The talking and sharing with others on the last day is also very important. So, please, if anyone wants to leave before the end, please come and speak to me, or some of those who are helping to run the course.'

Two days later, in the middle of the afternoon session, someone began to hyperventilate. It started like the soft rhythm of a steam train in the distance, but quickly became louder and louder until it filled the tent, super-charging the atmosphere with fear. The frantic breathing finally exploded into a spine chilling, gut wrenching, extremely primal scream. The screamer finished screaming, promptly keeled over and was hurriedly carried from the tent by the lungi clad workers. By now everyone was very edgy, there was a sense of things being out of control. That evening Goenka ended the silence early, and said he intended to finish the course a day early.

There was a gap of a couple of days before John Woodman was due to start his course. I stayed and helped clear up. John Woodman's course was to be in the house with around thirty people. Things settled down, the crowds left and only a core of old students remained. There was Rebecca from Israel, and a very sweet, young English girl called Roseanne, just out of school and very committed to meditation. They were both staying long term at the house, either sitting or serving courses. There was a lovely, motherly woman from Italy called Grazia who never seemed to meditate, but cooked wonderfully and radiated warmth and love. There was Swiss Thomas who I had met at Igatpuri. Laurie had told me with great delight about how Thomas had been thrown into confusion at Dharmagiri, after receiving a gift of a box of liqueur chocolates sent from Switzerland. We had all taken the eight precepts, one of which was to refrain from all intoxicants. So he could not eat them, and he could not give them away; that would be encouraging others to use intoxicants. In the end he had buried them. Then there was a central core of serious, old students who had been involved from the beginning, either with Goenka or Sayama. They were the main support for the house. Some lived locally, a few stayed long term at Splatts. One who was staying long term at the house was called Don. He sat at the front near the teachers, he never wobbled, and seemed to have no doubts at all. I too had my place at the fringe of Splatts House as a committed meditator, but I was young and inexperienced. I still had doubts, and I was prone to asking the wrong questions.

After John Woodman's course there was a gap of five days

before the course led by Mother Sayama began. I decided to have a break from the intensity of the centre, and went to visit Laurie at his parents' home in Hay-on-Wye. I hitch hiked, the day was sunny and I got lifts easily.

'I suppose you will be watching the wedding this afternoon?' asked one driver.

Wedding? I couldn't think what he was talking about.

'What wedding?' I asked.

'Prince Charles and Diana!' he replied in disbelief.

'Are they getting married today?' I asked, genuinely surprised, 'I didn't know.'

'You must be the only person in the whole country,' he replied.

Five days later I returned to sit my first course with Mother Sayama. Although Mother Sayama was sitting at the front, the course was led by her husband U Chit Tin. They looked like a very conventional, middle-aged, respectable Burmese couple. Mother Sayama sat and occasionally chanted, but all the instructions and talks were given by her husband U Chit Tin. His talks were full of references to traditional Burmese Theravadan Buddhism. As I listened to U Chit Tin's evening talks I realised that, for him, there was no separation between the Burmese Buddhist tradition he had grown up in and the meditation he taught. I wasn't sure if I was a Burmese Buddhist; my relationship with the Buddha and his teachings felt more direct, and I didn't want to belong to a particular sect. During the course I didn't experience any of the great insights I had fantasised that I might. I was disappointed in one way, but I knew that it wasn't meant to be like that; it was about a slow process of mental purification. But I still felt that true change would come suddenly, not gradually. It had to, logically it had to. There were also many stories I had heard about the experiences of the various teachers in Burma. These stories did not tell of gradual awakenings. It seemed people had spontaneous spiritual experiences, so always at the back of my mind when I sat, I was waiting for something to happen.

When the course was over I found myself talking with Thomas.

'Did you have a good course with Sayama and U Chit Tin?' he asked.

'Well yes,' I replied, 'but U Chit Tin's Dharma talks are certainly different to Goenkaji's.'

'Oh yes!' enthused Thomas, 'his connection to the scriptures is so wonderful.'

I found there was a letter waiting for me from my father. An old friend of his, who ran a Hotel Barge in central France, needed a boatman. I wasn't very sure if I wanted to go back into the intense and very uncontemplative life of Hotel barging. In the Buddhist sense of 'Right livelihood', catering to the over-indulged whims of wealthy American tourists didn't seem very wholesome, but it was work, and I needed the money.

I returned to England in the autumn. I had spent three months on the barge with my altar and Guru photos. I had read the story of Milarepa and wept at his devotion to Marpa his Guru. I had marvelled that in this day and age I, too, had a true Guru. Once the season was over on the barge I found myself directionless again. I had heard about a Rudolf Steiner community in Yorkshire, a residential care centre for the mentally handicapped. I wondered if it would be a place I could go, somewhere I could put a stop to my transient lifestyle. Another possibility that had been playing on my mind was going to Burma with Mother Sayama, to do what was called the Monk's Course. The monk's course was an ordinary meditation course, but was sat after one had become a fully ordained Buddhist monk. The ordination was temporary, lasting as long as the course. It had been hyped up at Splatts House; the strength of sitting at the U Ba Khin centre in Rangoon; the rare opportunity of being able to take robes. I had wondered if, perhaps, a big break through might happen to me there, as it had happened to others while they sat with U Ba Khin. Maybe this was my chance. Although I had wanted to become a monk, I was not very comfortable with the idea of becoming a monk for a few weeks, then disrobing after the course. It seemed a bit too quick to be meaningful, but I pushed these thoughts away.

When I got off the ferry from France I took a train west and went straight to Splatts House. I arrived to find there was a course led by Sayama in it's second day, and I decided to join it. I was asked to pay. This was new. So far all the time I had spent at the centres, both at Splatts House and in India, it had been on a donation basis. I was told apologetically that they now had to charge to be sure of covering costs. It was a modest amount and I didn't give it a lot of thought, it just seemed sad that things had not managed to work on a 'give as you can' basis. In the kitchen Grazia clapped her hands together with pleasure when I came in.

'Oh Ken ! You are back,' she said happily.

Don was sitting at the table.

'Hi Ken ,' he said coolly, 'how are you?'

I was shown my dormitory, then I was straight back into it. Silence, sitting, observing the body and mind.

After two or three days, during an after lunch rest, I was idly reading the main notice board. Reading and writing were not allowed during a course, so any printed words, even the fire instructions, suddenly seemed of great literary interest. At the top of the board there was a display entitled 'Teachers in the U Ba Khin Tradition.' I had looked at it many times before. There was a photo of U Ba Khin with lines drawn downwards to the present teachers. There was a photo of John Woodman and one of Mother Sayama, but where Goenka's picture had been there was now a gap. The pink card on which the photos were stuck revealed a light pink square where the photo had been removed, and the other photos moved around to disguise the fact. I looked around at the other notices. There was no mention of Goenka anywhere. There was no mention of Dharmagiri, or any of the other Goenka centres in India. According to the information board at Splatts House there was no one to teach, and no place to go to learn U Ba Khin Vipassana in the whole of India.

I went to the house office, an old caravan in the courtyard, where an old student was doing office work.

'Hi Ken ,' he asked, 'what can I do for you?'

'Well,' I began, 'I was just looking at the notice board and everything about Goenka has vanished. I'd like to know what's going on.'

His manner changed. He beckoned me to sit down, and became earnest and serious.

'You know Ken ,' he said taking a deep breath, 'you or I might sometimes get on an ego trip. That can happen. It can happen to anyone. But if it happens to someone in a position of authority, well, then it can be even stronger.'

He paused, as if trying to gather his thoughts.

He continued, 'And we cannot always understand things that may happen to other people.'

He looked at me hopefully.

I said, 'I don't really know what you are talking about.'

He looked at me with a confused pain in his eyes.

'You had better come and see U Chit Tin.'

I was taken to the top of the house to the rooms that had been converted into an apartment for Sayama and her husband. I was ushered into a room with several serious old students who suddenly seemed to be accompanying me.

U Chit Tin was quickly briefed, in muffled tones, about my question. I was directed to sit in front of him. U Chit Tin began talking.

'You see,' he said, 'one time the Buddha was sitting outside in the forest and Mara come to him. You know Mara?' he asked.

'Well, yes,' I said uneasily; Mara was the Buddhist equivalent of the devil.

U Chit Tin continued, 'The Buddha, he is like a rock, and Mara he come and smash!' He drove his hand down into his fist like a dive bombing aeroplane, 'Smash! and nothing happen because the Buddha is like a rock, and Mara have no power. You understand?' I nodded noncommittally.

'But we not strong like the Buddha. Eh?' asked U Chit Tin.

I nodded again.

'Sometime Mara come and people fall. When people get....' he hesitated, 'too big, then Mara come and this is very bad. When Sayama come back to Splatts house this summer she feel very bad vibrations from Mara. She not sleeping for many days! So now you understand?' he asked bluntly.

'Yes, I think I understand.' I said. I was getting the gist of it, but I found the fact he had not mentioned Goenka by name rather odd.

'Good,' said U Chit Tin, 'now you keep meditating, eh?'

Back in the office Don smoothly managed a more coherent explanation.

'We don't like to talk about it Ken, but it seems that Goenkaji has become carried away by being a Guru. After his course here this summer, when Mother Sayama came back, she could not sleep for ten days. The vibrations were so bad in the house. Because of this she has asked Goenkaji to stop giving such big courses, and to surrender to her as his teacher. She has also asked him to start charging for courses as we do now, in order to dissuade the wrong people from attending.

Unfortunately he has not complied with these conditions, and Mother Sayama has said he can no longer be considered a teacher in the U Ba Khin tradition.'

I remembered all the feelings I had had on the course in Jaipur. How I had seen Goenka as proud and arrogant, but then I had seen him as great and loving. Suppose those initial perceptions had been right?

'Does that mean I shouldn't sit with Goenka?' I asked anxiously.

'Well, we don't say that,' said Don with the air of a diplomat, 'you have to make up your own mind who is the right teacher for you.'

That seemed very weird. First I was told Goenka was completely off the rails, on a serious ego trip, possessed by the forces of Mara, and that after his course the vibrations were so bad that Anagami Mother Sayama couldn't sleep for ten days. But then it's up to me if I want to meditate with him?

I went back onto the course and tried to continue meditating but my mind was busy. It seemed as if all my initial doubts about Goenka had been given credence. And, apart from anything else, I was at Splatts house and Goenka was a long way away in India. I didn't know if I was going back to India. I felt vaguely abandoned. Every one, including Goenka, had said how spiritually developed Sayama was. Could I dismiss her advice, and if I could, then who could I believe? It seemed I would have to stay with Sayama. As for the rest of it, I would have to be my own master. I decided I did not need to believe in everything they believed in order to sit courses with them. So, before I left Splatts House, I put my name down on the list of those wishing to sit the monk's course.

I spent a few days with my parents then hitched to London. I rang Colin, an old friend from my art school days in Rugby. Occasionally I stayed at his flat when I was in London. Colin had gone from Rugby to Hornsey School of Art, and then onto the Royal Academy. Now he worked in the parks for Tottenham council and painted at night. He lived in a third story flat which was reached through a grim stairway, the carpets were threadbare, the walls peeling and filthy. Colin treated my periodic appearances with equanimity. This time he had a girl staying with him. Her name was Tali, she was from Israel and was a classical pianist. That evening we all went to the pub together. I talked about my ideas of going to work with the handicapped, but I did not mention going to Burma. I was having serious doubts, and had decided in the meantime to go back to Splatts house and sit another course with Mother Sayama to help clarify things.

'Well Ken , what do you think of my new friend?' asked Colin, looking at Tali, his eyes full of detached amusement. Tali smiled at me crazily.

'I think she is beautiful,' I said honestly, smiling crazily back.

'Oooh Ken!' cried Tali.

The next morning Tali came into the lounge where I was sleeping on the floor. Colin had gone to work, and I was planning to leave after breakfast.

'Ken,' said Tali softly, in a way that made my heart ache. I looked at her blearily from my sleeping bag.

'You are leaving today?' she asked shyly.

'Once I've had some breakfast.' I said.

'Ken, I want to come with you,' said Tali simply.

I felt a mixture of pleasure and confusion.

'But Tali, you don't even know where I am going!'

'I don't care', she said, 'I want to come.'

'What about Colin?' I asked, 'and anyway I'm going to a meditation centre. It's not like an ordinary place.'

'I don't mind, I come to a meditation centre,' she said, unwavering.

I explained to her that we would not be able to talk to each other, that if she came with me she would have to sit a meditation course, that it meant ten days of silence, ten days of sitting on a cushion. She would be alone. However, she was determined, and I was confused and a little frightened of her. Tali's inner pain had left many small scars on her arms and thick scars across her wrists. Yet if she wanted to come and sit a course and receive the teachings of the Buddha, I could hardly tell her not to. I believed it was the most valuable thing anyone could do. I thought maybe that was to be my role in her life. As we walked towards the station she tucked her arm through mine and hugged it. She put her head close to my shoulder.

'Ken,' she said, as if just for the pleasure of hearing the sound.

As I drank in the warmth of another person, a friend in my loneliness, alarm bells rang far away at the back of my mind.

Tali and I sat a retreat at Splatts house. She was treated kindly by the people at the house. She was taken care of by Israeli Rebecca, who by now had a budding, though very formal, love affair going on with Don. Through Rebecca, Don got to know Tali's story. By this time Don had been appointed an assistant teacher. He oozed an easy authority, like a Federal Agent. Tali was completely blown away by it all, and she thought they were all saints. Hugging me wildly at the end of the course she told me,

'Ken, I have something real now. You have given me a precious thing.'

A day or so after the retreat Don took me aside.

'Ken, I don't think you and Tali should stay here.'

I was shocked. What had we done?

'But why not?' I asked.

'I think you need to deal with what's going on between you both.'

'What do you mean?' I asked.

'Well Ken, everyone can feel it when you two are in the room together. The sexuality between you. I think you need to sort that out. This is not the place for that energy.'

Don was being up front.

'Why don't you go to a hotel in Chippenham,' he suggested.

I was astonished. I liked Tali. I had already half fallen in love with her, but, as much as anything out of a loyalty to Colin, I hadn't been thinking about sleeping with her. It was embarrassing to be told that we were creating public sensations, and then to be sent off to fuck in a hotel. I talked to Tali.

'Don says we should leave. He says the sexual energy around us is so strong everyone else can feel it.'

'Oooh Ken!' said Tali, and we hugged each other laughing crazily, and then suddenly and intensely, I felt it too.

We booked into a bed and breakfast hotel in Chippenham, just as Don had said we should. It was hygienically clean, decorated in whites and pinks. There was a restaurant with white china cats on lace doilies where we sat whispering, drinking tea from pointy cups. In the bedroom Tali got undressed and lay on the bed. I did the same. I tried to kiss her but Tali turned away.

'No kissing!' said Tali, 'just make love to me.'

She lay back expectantly. I had been virtually celibate for the four years since parting with Kate. Sex was scary, full of potential pain, I was too tense. I was in love with Tali, I wanted to cuddle her and kiss her, I wanted to become close to her then make love with her, not suddenly have to fuck her in this horrible prissy hotel. I felt I just couldn't do it, but Tali wanted to be had, to be taken with an urgency that froze me.

Later, as we lay in a cold cloud of frustration, there was a creak of floor boards outside the door, and we realised someone had been watching through the key hole. We left and caught the bus back to London. We didn't speak much on the journey, Tali was quiet, withdrawn into herself. When we got out of the tube station near to Colin's flat she turned to me.

'Don't come with me Ken,' she said, 'I have to see Colin alone.'

I looked through my address book and found the number of a couple I'd met that summer at Splatts House. I rang them, it was eight thirty in the evening and raining. They had trouble remembering who I was but, repressing their obvious irritation, told me to come on over. I slept on the floor in the small room they used for meditation. At one in the morning. tormented, I rang Colin's number. The phone rang for an eternity. Finally, Colin's voice, befuddled and sleepy was in my ear.

'Hello, who is it?' he asked.

'It's Ken,' I said, then asked,' are you with Tali?'

He knew what I was asking.

'Yes,' he answered simply and emotionlessly.

I was silent. There was nothing to say.

'Are you all right?' he asked.

A few days later I was back sitting another course at Splatts House. When it was over I was told that, although it had been touch and go, I was to be allowed to go to Burma to sit the monk's course. I was asked to pay two hundred pounds in advance to pay for administration charges and to purchase our monks robes. It seemed a lot. I went back to my parents' house to sort things out for the trip via London, where I met up with Laurie. Laurie had been at Splatts house that summer while I was in France. He had seen the split between Goenka and Sayama as it happened, and he gave me the background details. It had all started two years earlier. Sayama and U Chit Tin had come to Dharmagiri in India at Goenka's invitation. Unfortunately Mother Sayama, or U Chit Tin, had not liked the way things were going with Goenka in India. When they had last seen him he had been a student of U Ba Khin's. Now they found him as the big teacher with his own centre, leading courses of two or three hundred students, much bigger than any courses led by U Ba Khin. Goenka had also instigated the payment by donation, and Sayama, or U Chit Tin, thought this accounted for the large numbers that came to his courses. So things had been tense long before the meeting at Splatts house. It seemed odd that those teaching Vipassana meditation as a method of seeing the truth, including one who was supposed to be virtually enlightened, could not even communicate or come to an understanding. It was not a very good advertisement for the technique, especially all the secrecy and unwillingness to talk openly about what was going on.

'If my Dharma parents are getting a divorce,' said Laurie, 'I want to be told what is going on, not treated like I don't need to know!'

His irreverence was joyful after the piety of Splatts House. The trouble was I was going to Burma. I had invested too much in going there to change my mind. I was tired of suffering and confusion. I wanted sudden enlightenment, and for any chance of that I was willing to suspend my misgivings.

When I got home to my parents house I found out that my brother, who was living in Florida, was getting married. I was being offered a free, round trip, with a three week stay, and enticing offers of female companionship. But my tickets to Burma were booked, I had my visa, it was too late to stop. It had begun to feel like my last chance for peace.

Chapter 9

BURMA 1982

Bangladesh Biman flight 304 was delayed for two hours by technical problems, an improbable sounding, 'Pilot's oxygen bottle.' I sat in the Heathrow departure lounge surrounded by the ten members of my group. I had never travelled in a group before. The train and bus journey, instead of being a time of solitary reflection and observation, had been an embarrassing circus. The louder members of the group had drawn the attention of the whole carriage by brashly calling out unnecessary advice. 'Hey you guys! There are four seats here! Put that big case by the door.' Once we were all seated there was more jolly banter and excited speculation about what lay ahead. I had found myself travelling with the last of three groups from Splatts House. It seemed as if we had gone in some kind of hierarchical order, with the most senior and most devoted students going first. My group seemed to be made up of the weirdos and misfits. The self-appointed group leader was a Dutch man called Hans. Getting ready at the house Hans brought each of us a carrier bag of things to hide in our luggage.

'If you are asked anything at customs,' he told me enthusiastically, 'just say it is Sangha Dana.

Sangha Dana meant donations for the community of monks. I looked at the contents of the carrier bag and then, unhappily, began to push the expensive bottles of Oil of Ulay face cream and Camay leather soap into my well worn, grubby pack. It seemed a funny kind of Sangha Dana. I felt more like a courier.

At Heathrow airport I began again to mull over the words in the I Ching- 'If the little fox rushes ahead onto the thin ice, then all is lost.' All is lost! Did it mean going to Burma? Did it mean the plane would crash? Was I in the wrong place? I didn't want to be with these people, I only wanted to get away from them. Yet I could not act, I no longer knew which of my feelings I should trust. I wondered if I should just get up and go. There was still time. But then, what? I might realise I really should be going to Burma, that this was a one off chance. And even if I did want to stay in England, I had nowhere to go. My family were all in Florida for my brother's wedding, I had no key to the house, nowhere else to stay and nothing to do. So I sat in the departure lounge, thoughts raging, paralysed by uncertainty.

We boarded the plane. It was a wreck. There were patches on the wings. The upright position on my seat was faulty and I kept crashing back. The tray in front of me periodically popped down by itself. There seemed to be far more people than seats, and massive amounts of excess baggage. I felt sure we were all about to die. Finally we were careering down the runway. Fear exploded through my body. I tried to meditate, to observe the fear as sensation, but that only made it worse. We left the ground and, amazingly, carried on going up. I looked out of the window at the receding lights of Slough and Reading. The plane settled down, I settled down and the passengers all started to get up. It was like being in a Bangladeshi railway carriage. There were old men with beards and skull caps, young men in Saturday-Night-Fever suits, clutching improbably large tape recorders, women in saris holding crying babies, and dozens of beautiful children dashing between the seats. Later in the flight, in a toilet queue, I chatted with an over made-up girl in tight jeans and a Birmingham accent.

'I've never been there before,' she said, wanting me to know where she stood on the cultural issue, 'it's me folks, you see. They wanted me to go and see it all. But what am I going to do in a village of mud houses? I shall probably die of boredom. Where are you going?' she asked.

'I'm going to Burma to... er, study Buddhism.'

She looked at me, categorising me anew.

'You into all religious stuff then?' she asked.

'Well I suppose....'

Then the toilet door opened and she was gone. Dawn brought us to Dacca and then onto Rangoon. The low sun caught the snaking rivers below us, connecting and inter-connecting in a tangle of water ways, as much water as land. The airport building was straight out of the colonial past. No plate glass and ferrous concrete, it was all white paint, verandas and flag poles. There was trouble at customs when one of the bigger trunks revealed its haul of cosmetics.

'Sangha Dana! Sangha Dana!' cried Hans, idiotically to the unflinching customs officer. We had been met by someone from the centre, and after a while we were let through, no doubt a few Oil of Ulay bottles lighter.

The U Ba Khin meditation centre was built on and around a small hill in the suburbs of the city. Like the surrounding properties, the buildings were single storied with wide verandas. The garden was dusty, full of large flowering bushes and trees. On the top of the hill was the pagoda topped by a thick golden spire, surrounded by meditation cells. Next to the pagoda was the meditation hall, a roof with timber framed walls covered with wire mesh to allow the air to flow through. The new monks from Splatts house stood around looking self consciously mindful. After paying our respects to Mother Sayama in the meditation hall, I was shown where I would sleep. I was to share a six bed simple concrete building with three others. We had a crude shower and toilet. When my guide had gone I put my bag on the bed, went into the toilet and threw up. Soon the bell was ringing for the evening meditation. I wanted to go straight to bed, but no one else talked of tiredness. There was no mention of jet lag or an early night for the newcomers. I dragged myself to the meditation hall. As soon as the meditation session began I fell asleep. I was woken by the sensation of falling forward, I stopped just before my nose hit the floor. I sat up, took a deep breath, and instantly fell asleep. I woke with the floor a few inches in front of my face, so I sat up again. I continued this for the whole hour; it was like being suspended by elastic. Several times, as I pulled myself back up, I noticed Mother Sayama watching me.

After the sitting, to my surprise, I felt better. I walked for a while through the tropical night. I was looking for a familiar face, someone I could talk to. As I passed by the students who were now in robes, I realised how few of them I knew. When I got back to the hall little Roseanne was there, sweet and earnest, sitting on the flat paved area around the pagoda. She was looking after registration. She asked me how long I wished to stay. I had started thinking about staying three weeks then flying on to India. I had fantasies of doing a retreat alone in the mountains. But when she asked, my fantasies dissolved. I had already surrendered too much of myself by just getting on the plane. I had exchanged what little will I had left for the hope of salvation. To go on alone from this place was suddenly unimaginable. I told her I wanted to stay in Burma, at the centre, for as long as I could. She looked quietly pleased; this was the right answer, I was showing I was serious.

'While you are here you will not be able to leave the compound,' she told me, 'those are the conditions of the long stay permits.'

'Right, that's okay,' I said, and handed over my passport.

The next morning I was given Burmese clothes to wear, the uniform I had always disliked. Before becoming fully ordained monks or Bhikkhus, we had to become samanera or novice monks. This was intended as a preparatory period before taking the full commitment of monkshood. Aspirants would normally be samaneras for one or two years, while we were to be samanera for about twenty four hours.

The first ceremony we had to take part in was the taking of the precepts. Our preceptor was an elderly Burmese monk. He had arrived earlier with a party of four younger monks. They had been received with much bowing and reverence which was accepted with, what seemed to me, to be casual indifference. I noticed there were no young Burmese people at the centre. They were all middle aged or older. The young people were westerners. We were made to wait in a line. The old monk remained in the hall while the young monks came outside and opened up the small cases they were carrying. Inside, the metal glinting, were cut throat razors. Two chairs were brought and put in the shade. Then we were called forward in turn, two at a time, and with two monks for each head, we had our heads shaved. There was no time for second thoughts. The Burmese women gathered to watch like proud grandmothers at a school sports day. It was grotesque, almost disgusting. The long curls of wet hair peeled off the pasty white heads like the skin off some foul fruit. Rebecca and Roseanne were taking photos and joining in with the celebratory atmosphere. I did not share this feeling at all, I felt as though I were being abused.

Later we sat, like political prisoners, in front of our preceptor, in order according to age. I was the youngest monk. The preceptor then began the formal introduction to the monastic life. This took a long time as all he said had to be translated sentence by sentence. It was completely meaningless. Except for a few basic details, it had nothing to do with the life we would be leading at the centre. At the end of the ceremony we were handed what looked like a new, dark orange, double duvet set. The four head shavers began to show us how to wear our new garments. There were two robes; a lower robe that served as a lungi, which was wrapped around the waist, with the surplus material folded into an S shape, and held at the front by a webbed belt. The second robe was wrapped around the upper body, sexily revealing one shoulder. I found wearing the robes a bit erotic, which without underpants was rather alarming. We were then given our new names. I became Dharmananda, he who loves the Dharma. So far it was the only thing I felt good about.

The next day, after a breakfast of oily sticky noodles and chewy meat, we were loaded into cars. We were off to become monks. We drove through the outskirts of the city, water buffalo meandered in stone pools by decaying temples, small elegant women walked along the road sides wearing brightly coloured, tight fitting lungis, happy children played in the dust. I realised I had no passport, it had been taken away. I had no money or possessions, these too had been taken away, I had no hair, no friends and I felt like a prisoner being transported between jails. The monastery was down a side street, and was a collection of decaying buildings. We were taken into a large hall with an oversized Buddha statue at one end. The hall looked as though it had not been used for years. A dim light shone through the boarded up windows onto the Buddha who stared, unseeing, into the dusty gloom. In one corner there was a wooden bed and an ancient, glass fronted book case with newspaper, gone orange with age, glued and peeling from the glass. Accumulated junk was piled on top.

Our preceptor and his monks went and sat in front of the Buddha statue facing us. This time we were called forward in groups of three for questioning, which as before, was all done laboriously through an interpreter. I was put together with another young Englishman called Chris. There were long stretches of chanting by the monks, and other chants we had to repeat. There were questions we had to answer, as directed, 'No Sir,' or 'Yes Sir,' in Burmese. One of the questions was, 'Are you a human being?' Chris and I exchanged humorous looks, it was like being kids at school. One of the serious old students, who was already a monk, was there to help out. He seemed very tense compared to the Burmese monks. They lounged at the back punctuating their conversation with well aimed shots at the spittoon. They looked bored. One of them casually swatted a mosquito, then flicked the squashed remains off his robes. The two Burmese meditation teachers from the U Ba Khin centre sat at the far end of the hall by the door, reading newspapers and smoking cigarettes. They looked as if they were waiting for their car to be fixed. When it was all over we were fully ordained Buddhist monks.

When we arrived back at the meditation centre one of the other old students, already a monk, came up to me. He looked dreamily at me.

'So,' he asked, 'how does it feel to be a Bhikkhu?'

'Well,' I replied honestly, 'I can't say I feel much different.'

'When I put the robes on,' he said, 'it felt so natural, so familiar. I felt...' he hesitated, '...so at peace.'

I wandered off struggling with 'negative feelings'. Back at the dormitory I found Chris sitting outside.

'So Bhikkhu,' I asked repeating the question, 'how does it feel to be a Bhikkhu? Something more than a new hair cut and wearing an orange duvet cover?'

Chris laughed, 'I don't know what I expected to feel, something more special, perhaps.'

I was seriously regretting having come to Burma. I felt the ritualised monkshood made a mockery of the real thing. I could hardly believe I had chosen to get involved. Back in England, one of the Splatts House groupies while extolling the virtues of the monk's course, had told me how at the time of

Maitreya, the next Buddha, only those who had been monks in previous lives would be able to join him. The belief that this quality could be reduced to a ritual, a quick two week investment for another life, was surprising to me. Yet I had come, in the hope that this special place, this special course, would be where I could get to the root of it all. It would be where I went beyond. But I wasn't getting beyond, I was just getting deeper in.

As everyone had said it was very 'strong' sitting at the centre, especially as a monk, I decided to try and forget about my objections to the Burmese Buddhist trimmings. I would, as the jargon went, just make best use of the rare opportunity. But my meditation was awful. My mind was a chaotic stream of thoughts, doubts and misgivings, and it was impossible to concentrate. I took breaks to smoke cigarettes and try to clear my mind. Unlike the other centres there was no 'Noble silence', and also smoking was allowed. I wandered around for the time it took to consume a duty free Marlborough, then returned, unrefreshed, to my cell. It felt odd to have a break for a smoke, rather like a builder. My thoughts raged on, round and round. Should I be in India? Should I be with Goenka, not Sayama? Could I trust Goenka? Should I disrobe and get out? Could I leave the centre as a monk and just wander off and live by begging?

In the evening we met with Mother Sayama. She asked us about our meditation.

'Concentration good?' she asked me.

'A lot of thoughts,' I said.

She looked at me intently, I thought she looked worried.

Later I tried to discuss my feelings with one of the Burmese teachers called U Chit Tee, he had sat reading the paper at the precept ceremony. He listened as I stumbled out my doubts about being a monk. I tried to present them as cautious enquires rather than outright arguments.

'The Dharma is the teaching of the Buddha. Practising the Dharma is what you are doing here,' he told me, 'and the best way to practice the Dharma is as a monk.'

It sounded so simple. He was kind, fatherly and as he talked I realised he knew nothing of my inner turmoil. I suspected he had never ever had doubts at all. There was so much I wanted to be able to talk about, but as he spoke I knew there was no way I could. Coming to Burma was beginning to feel a complete disaster. I was in the wrong place with the wrong people. The little fox had rushed ahead, the thin ice had broken, and all was lost.

After the evening group sitting in the hall I felt calmer. I felt sad, exhausted and longed for the comfort and oblivion of sleep. I brushed my teeth at the concrete wash basin in the dim orange glow of the one light bulb. Mosquitoes whined around my head. I went to my wooden bed and carefully tucked the mosquito net under the paper thin rush mat that served as a mattress, then I fell into an exhausted sleep. I woke in the middle of the night, anxiety and fear rushed into me like evil spirits. To calm myself I got up and went out into the night and smoked a couple of cigarettes. It was one a.m. I walked around the Pagoda for a while, and noticed lights on in the Dharma hall. The source of light was the shrine at the back. I sat in front of it and looked at the Buddha statue, but it seemed foreign, not the Buddha I knew. There was a shrine for U Ba Khin, and I looked at his photo. It struck me that U Ba Khin had not doubted Goenka, and I felt a bond with the old man. At least there was one person I could trust.

In the meditation cell throughout the next days I sat and dozed off. It was like being drugged. As soon as I began to watch my breath it was like being gassed. Each time I fell asleep I fell forward, I awoke, and realised what had happened, but the moment I watched a few breaths I was gone again. I knew this was not tiredness, it was avoidance. I had started to formulate a plan about going to India after Burma, and spent a lot of time refining the details. It became my refuge and escape, it made me feel good and above all it kept me awake. I drifted through a haze of sleepiness and thoughts as the days slipped by. In my diary I wrote out many of my thoughts in an attempt to make order of them. I wrote nothing about what I would have described as my negative feelings about the place and people. Instead I analysed all I felt in terms of meditation. I was experiencing the five main hindrances to meditation. I could remember three, sceptical doubt, discursive thinking and craving and aversion, but I could not remember the other two. I went to find Thomas because I knew he studied the scriptures.

'Thomas', I asked, 'what are the Five Hindrances?'

Instead of answering my question, he replied, patronisingly, 'why do you want to know?'

'None of your bloody business!' I snapped.

Every few days our preceptor came to the centre and we had to go through a ritualised confessional with him. We sat in front of him and read the confession from a piece of paper in Burmese. We were told to keep in our minds any infringements of the rules we had made while we spoke. As a confessional I thought it was a bit of a cop-out, not that there was much to confess anyway, cocooned as we were within the centre. One afternoon we were told we were being taken to a large temple for a special full moon confession. The temple was set in a beautiful garden next to a lake, with a circular hall in which we sat. The evening light caught the trees and grass, turning them golden. The hall was warm and rang with the chanting of the monks. I sat there in my robes and felt the beauty of what I was missing. I wanted to stay in that hall, wrapped in saffron, gone forth from the world. I didn't want to go back.

As the days went by I became increasingly depressed. I felt filled with pride and selfishness. I had taken my father's hard earned money so I could stay in India and indulge in a spiritual fantasy. I had stayed in his house, and then only criticised and judged him and my mother. And all for what? What had I achieved? What had I become? I was vain, insecure, deluded. Suddenly the fact I had not gone to my brother's wedding hit me with the intensity of a broken heart. How could I have not gone? I had turned my back on the people who loved me. I could hardly bear to think it about it, and longed to ask their forgiveness. I felt determined to become a better person. I made a new plan. I would go back to England, live at my parents' house and work to save money. In the autumn I would return to Burma for a month long course. After that I would go to India and spend the winter in a cave. While I lived at home I would be ever watchful of the arising of Lobha, lust, Moha, hatred and Dosha, ignorance. I had been reading about these defilements from the Buddhist books at the centre. I would meditate every day, I would be very calm and loving and bring happiness into my parents' lives. With this new plan I felt grateful I was in a place where I could understand so much about human unhappiness, and be able to purify my mind by meditating.

I spent a lot of time refining this plan, working out the details. When I stopped fantasising and applied myself to being aware of sensations in the present I fell asleep. One day, during a usual sleepy meditation, I felt my body lift into a very upright position. My back became straight, as if of it's own accord, until I was sitting very upright and very still. Then, quite unexpectedly, a sudden rush of energy was released from the base of my spine. It shot upwards, covering me in goose pimples, and burst into my head filling me with blissful joy and calm. After the meditation period was over I stood outside. Another meditator walked past me, stopped and came back. 'What happened to you?' he asked, 'you look completely different'. Yet when I returned to my cell for the next sitting I found, rather disappointingly, I just fell back into the usual slumped sleepy haze. I spoke to one of the teachers about my sleepiness and was told not to worry about it. The strength of the place brought so much up that if I had constant concentration it would be too much. It would blow my mind.

Towards the end of the monk's course, after an evening group sitting in the Pagoda, we were all asked to leave, except Don. He who had sent me off with Tali. He stayed in the Pagoda all evening with Sayama.

'Don is going very deep,' I was told, 'when people go very deep in their meditation, Mother Sayama works with them, and she can guide them into the Nirvanic state. It is possible to actually dip into Nirvana for a few moments.'

Then later the word went around in hushed excitement.

'Don's dipped!' they cried, 'Don's dipped!'

The monk's course ended simply, a five minute formality with our preceptor. It was a relief to get my own clothes back. Little Roseanne brought me photo's of myself as a monk. When she had gone I tore them up and threw them in the bin. I didn't want any spiritual souvenirs. The other meditators put on a new uniform, traditional Burmese lungi and shirt; some of the keener, old students also dressed in the cotton jacket worn by respectable Burmese gentlemen. I put on my old, baggy army trousers and a well worn T shirt, An old student came by with a drab lungi for me, and politely asked me to take my clothes off, and wear the lungi.

I stayed for another four weeks at the centre, sitting for most of the time. I was left alone, not fitting in with the Sayama devotees. I settled down as a misfit, and became used to the painful contents of my head. As the time to leave came closer I began to let go of my plans to become a Good Buddhist Son. I began to realise just how glad I would be to get away from the place. Many times I had wanted to leave but I had been scared. I was deeply superstitious, and I wanted to leave with the group I had come with. This was not because I felt any affection for them, but simply because of the sense I had of being on the wrong part of the planet at the wrong time. I thought their plane was less likely to crash. I wanted to hitch a ride on their good Karma. So I stayed and continued sitting week after week. I dreamed my dreams and the days passed by. Finally the last day came and, with seven others, I flew back to Heathrow and took the train to Splatts House. The next morning I collected the things I had left there and said good-bye to everyone.

'See you soon,' they said, 'see you on the next course.'

But I never went back or saw any of them again, except Chris, who I met years later in robes. He had become a real Buddhist monk.

I arrived in London in early March, the city was bleak and cold. I decided to look up Duncan, who had sailed to Europe on the Malaysian junk from Bombay. He had been living in a squat in Islington, but when I arrived I found he had left a few weeks earlier for India. His girlfriend was still there and she invited me to stay. I liked the people who lived in the squat. They were refreshingly normal, without piety. On the second day, as I sat in the kitchen and looked out over the wet London roof tops, I resolved that, if I could, I would stay there. I would stop travelling aimlessly about, living on other peoples hospitality. It was time to stop wandering, ever searching, it was time to apply myself. To become part of a community. I would settle down.

There was a room free, and I so stayed. I tried to find work, but I was without any skill or training so I lived off the dole. But instead of feeling settled I found the opposite. I lived with constant anxiety. I meditated every day, but unlike in the fantasy it did not lead to a calm peaceful life. It just meant I spent two hours each day sitting on a cushion, and if I managed to stop the anxieties and fears for a few moments during those two hours, it did nothing to stop them the rest of the time.

During my first weeks living in the squat my brother phoned from the south of France, and offered me the job of boatman on the hotel barge he was captaining. As I had decided that I needed to settle down, and his offer meant packing up and becoming homeless again, I nearly went mad with indecision. In the end I had turned the job down. I was the only member of the house out of work, so I was alone all day. I began writing about the year I had spent in India. I wrote hundreds of pages, hunched over my table, living on strong sweet tea and duty free cigarettes. I felt I had lost everything. This was where I had ended up after all my travelling. This was the end of the road. I was an untrained, unemployable, no-hoper living on state benefits in a crummy squat. I had lost a lot of weight and felt weak. I began to get pains in my chest. Then the pains became worse, and started to be accompanied by waves of cold that left me shivering and drained. I noticed my shit had turned oily black. One evening a girl who was studying osteopathy visited the squat.

'What does it mean if you have really black shit?' I asked her, somewhat embarrassed.

'It can mean,' she answered carefully, 'that you are bleeding internally.'

The next morning I packed an old suitcase with my books and writings, packed my rucksack and, summoning all my reserves of energy, I set off to Euston station. It was a half mile walk. I struggled with the desire to lie down on the pavement, to give up. Three hours later I was back in my parents' spare bedroom. I pulled off my clothes and fell into bed. The room was quiet, the sheets were cool and clean, the bed felt as comfortable as a womb. Gratefully I fell into a deep and dreamless sleep. The next day at Northampton hospital I waited for my gastroscopy. I refused the injections of valium, seriously believing that it would affect my meditation. I knew I was to have an optical fibre put down my throat, but what I didn't know was that the fibre was in a tube the size of a shower hose. By the time I saw it, it was too late. The nurses held me while the doctor stuffed it down.

'Swallow! Swallow!' he cried.

I swallowed and the ghastly pipe slid down. I gagged and writhed uncontrollably. The nurses held me and the doctor began his inspection. In the middle, as I writhed, he asked enthusiastically,

'Would you like to have a look at your insides?'

In reply I tried to pull the pipe out. The nurses leapt forward and restrained me. When it was over the doctor came out to where I sat, stunned.

'You have three severe duodenal ulcers,' he told me, 'and you are very lucky that they did not haemorrhage. If they had, you might not be sitting here now.'

I spent the next weeks taking day long walks and eating well. I could see I had come to be in quite a mess. It seemed absurd, mad, to have got ulcers from a quest for inner peace. But as crazy as it was I could see no way out, attempting to settle down had nearly killed me, it seemed I could only go on. Goenka was coming to the south of France to lead a course in an old chateau in the Provence. Laurie and I decided to travel down together. Then my brother called again. Their boatman was leaving in three weeks. He offered me the job again, and this time I accepted, even though it meant I would not be able to sit the Goenka course.

A few weeks later Laurie and I rumbled down to Dover on a smoking wreck of a bus. We went by foot onto the ferry. At Calais we were met by a bus that seemed to be constructed from plate glass, and in this piece of mobile architecture we hissed south to Nice on the Riviera. We hitch hiked up into the hills behind to the small village where the course was to be held. As we walked the last miles, a battered Mercedes with German plates pulled up, and a blond head with perfect Teutonic chiselled features appeared out of the driver's window.

'Hey, Laurie! You want a lift!'

It was Klaus, a friend of Laurie's. I had met him several times over the past few years at Goenka courses. He and I had both started on the same course, and we'd both been friends with Laurie. Unknown to me, as I had set off to hitch hike north after my first course, Laurie had arranged to travel north with Eva. They had even got as far as buying the train tickets but, at the last moment, Eva had decided to stay and sit the next course. Typical Eva. Laurie had ended up taking the train to Delhi with Klaus. Klaus had been mad. He had been brought by his girlfriend from a junkie chaos in Goa to sit a ten day course. After the course he had a hard time, convinced everyone was out to rip him off, convinced he was dying of cancer. Laurie had stayed with him, allowing him to be mad, discussing and rediscussing the likelihood of his symptoms being of tumours or muscular dystrophy, able to accept his craziness, even liking him for it. Now, three years later, Klaus was a devoted Goenka student. Over the previous three years he had, like me, sat dozens of courses. It had changed his life. We squashed into the already full Mercedes and drove the last two miles up a dusty lane, pulling up finally outside a rambling chateaux that looked half derelict.

'Far out,' said someone in the front.

We had arrived a day early, but so had many others. Travellers were rolling in with scruffy clothes and backpacks from all over Europe. There were a lot of familiar faces from India. We slept out on the hillside under the olive trees for the first night, sharing our food and stories. These people were my Sangha, my Dharma community. When Goenka arrived the next day Laurie and I asked if we could have a meeting with him. I had to leave the next day to start work on the barge, and I wanted to see him before I left. We were shown into his room. He was resting, lying with his wife in a large bed, both propped up by a heap of pillows. We came in, unsure of where to sit. Goenka directed us to sit cross-legged beside the bed.

'Sit, sit,' he said, smiling benignly, 'so how are you both? You have a question?'

Laurie dived straight in.

'Goenkaji, last year we were both at Splatts House during the split between you and Sayama, and basically we would like to know how you see all that has happened.'

Goenka looked at the ceiling for a few moments.

'It has been a very difficult time for all of us. These things are very unfortunate,' he sighed, 'you see, many people come to me for courses, making the courses very big. In one way this is good, it means many people receive the Dharma and that is what Sayagi U Ba Khin, my teacher, wanted. As many as possible to benefit from the practice. Unfortunately, with such large numbers there are inevitably some difficult people, people who are psychologically unstable.' He paused.

Then he continued, 'Sayama has asked me to do things which contradict what I understood to be the wishes of Sayaji U Ba Khin. What I have been saying to people who come and ask me about these matters is that you have to choose who is the teacher for you. I am not saying people should not sit with

Sayama, I have great respect for Sayama, but I am saying choose who is the right teacher for you, and then work with that teacher.'

He waited to see if we had any questions. Laurie asked the question on every one's mind, but few had even put into words.

'Goenkaji. I have another question. How can this happen? You are both Dharma teachers. You have been meditating for many years. It is not a very good advertisement for the practice.'

It was clear Goenka had not expected this question. He looked surprised, then he waited, as if deciding just how much he was going to let on.

'It does not help now to lay blame at anyone's door. We must leave it behind. It does not benefit anyone to go on about these matters. Let us put it behind us. We need to purify our minds from old Sankaras, not make more. Do not dwell on this matter. Let it rest.'

I still respected Goenka. I knew that he had been my teacher, and I would still sit courses with him, but his answer to Laurie's second question did not remove my doubts. It was not that I doubted him; I didn't, I trusted him as a person, but I had lost my faith in the technique and the teachers' understanding of the path, I felt they had both failed me. I still wanted to meditate though, I still wanted to find out, to understand. But now I knew, I was on my own.

I spent the next few months working on the canals, and then picking grapes. I was far from being at peace. I was staying with some friends of friends who lived on a vineyard in the Dordogne. The day after the grape picking had finished Laurie rang. I was surprised he had managed to find out where I was. On the phone he was business like.

'Ken. I'm going back to India. I want to be out of the country by the tenth of October. What I want to know is, should I wait for you?'

'Okay,' I said, thrown by having to make such a decision, still rolling options around in my head. Go? Stay? Go? Stay?

'I'll be back by Wednesday. I'll meet you in London and we can get our tickets together,' I said with a certainty I did not feel.

'It will be good to see you again,' he said.

A week later I was back at my parents' house. Laurie and I had bought tickets to Karachi. The flight left in five days, and I was beginning to have the same old doubts.

What was I doing?

Why on earth was I going back to India?

Why?

It was a question I still couldn't answer. I talked to my parents. My mother thought I would be better off staying in England. My father remained detached.

'Ken,' he said, looking out of the window, 'I have no wisdom for you.'

Indecision filled my waking hours. I remembered how I had gone to Burma when I should have stayed in England, but then I had stayed in London when I should have gone to the barge. Was I going to India for meditation? And if I was, what kind of fantasy was that? Hadn't I tried that?

So I threw the I Ching. Instead of the hexagram entitled 'Before Completion,' with the warning of the little fox rushing ahead on thin ice, I got the one called, 'After Completion.'

'The time of transition from confusion to order is completed,' it said, *'there is a favourable outlook...'*

It sounded good but didn't help much. Finally with only a day left the indecision became intolerable. I forced myself to think it through rationally. It was obvious that I should stay in England and find something useful to do with my life, India was just a distraction. I had made up my mind, and before it could change I rang Laurie in London.

'Hello Laurie,' I said, 'I've decided not to go to India.'

'Well fuck you!' said Laurie.

I was shocked by his anger.

'I suppose you don't want to hear my reasons,' I said, suddenly knowing they would sound completely absurd if I told him.

'Not particularly,' he replied.

I wished him well and hung up. I told my parents what I had done then went up to bed. I lay in the darkness and realised Laurie was the only friend I had, he was the only person who understood. He was my brother in the Dharma and I had turned away from him. My indecision returned with a vengeance. Finally, in desperation, before I fell asleep I made a prayer to all the invisible forces of the Buddha Dharma.

'Help me please!' I thought as loudly as I could, 'I don't know what I should do, whether I should go to India or stay in England. Please show me in a dream tonight what I should do.'

The next morning when I awoke I realised I had had a most vivid dream. I had been standing on the third story of a burnt out house. The floor boards were burnt through, only the beams remained, spanning the gaping hole below. Balancing on one of these narrow charred beams I had crossed over one floor to a doorway in a dividing wall. There, between the gulf behind and the gulf ahead, I was gripped by fear and clung to the door frame. Laurie, who had come across behind, suddenly appeared beside me and put a warm and comforting hand on my shoulder.

'Go on Ken,' he said, 'cross over, don't be afraid.'

I leapt from my bed, rushed downstairs and burst into the dining room. My parents were having breakfast.

'I'm going to India!' I cried joyfully.

'Oh dear,' said my mother looking anxious.

Oh yes?' said my father rather doubtfully, over the top of his newspaper.

And suddenly I loved them both wildly.

Chapter 10

Laurie and I sat on either side of the chaotic compartment. Coolies passed tin trunks, rolls of bedding and boxes of consumer durables through the window. The other occupants seemed to be constantly changing, and everyone was talking at once. There were twenty minutes until the twenty four hour Karachi Lahore express was due to depart. Karachi had none of the faded elegance of Delhi and the other, once great, Indian cities. It was an isolated port suddenly promoted by the creation of Pakistan. At the station Laurie and I had got a shock.

'Two tickets on tomorrow's train to Lahore,' I asked.

'The train is fully booked for two weeks,' the clerk told us, vaguely contemptuous.

'Two weeks! But we are tourists,' I cried, 'we can't wait here two weeks.'

The clerk just shrugged his indifference.

'What about tourist quota?'

'No tourist quota,' he said with pleasure.

Faced with the prospect of two weeks in Karachi I did something I had never done before, I played the white Sahib.

'Then I want to see your superior officer,' I said, haughtily.

The clerk eyed us up, as if deciding whether he could call our bluff. With a scowl he turned and spoke to one of his colleagues. A few moments later we were shown, resentfully, into a large office where we were met by an urbane man in a blazer sporting a curly moustache.

'Do come in and sit down,' he said, 'would you care to take tea?'

We sat with our cups of tea and talked about our pressing

schedule, international cricket and how much we liked Pakistan. He agreed we couldn't possibly stay in Karachi for two weeks; the tickets would not be a problem. We thanked him but he dismissed our thanks.

'Not at all, my dear chaps,' he replied.

As he escorted us out, now with our reserved tickets for the following day, I caught the eye of the ticket clerk; his look was murderous.

A colour television was hoisted through the window inches from my nose and up onto the luggage rack, then a beaming baby was passed out onto the platform. It was a carnival, a party, the other children wanted to come through the windows, so they too were passed into the compartment and fussed over. The bigger bundles and tin trunks had to be jammed under the bench seats.

There were family members squatting on the floor, perched on the bedding bundles, standing in the aisles and they were all talking, shouting and laughing. Not long now. There was an old man in blue, with a gold skull cap and a long white beard. His wife sat next to him, invisible within her long black chador. The fans rattled wildly as if about to fly off their mountings. Laurie was talking to the young men in western clothes, who translated for two old ladies who in turn laughed and smiled. Then things began to settle down, money changed hands, the coolies wandered away counting and recounting their wads of grubby notes. The old man in the gold skull cap was touching the heads of the young men giving parting advice and instructions. They listened, nodding seriously as he spoke. It needed no translating.

'Mahmood, look after your wife well.'

'Yes sir.'

'Ali. You are a good boy. Your father is proud of you.'

'Thank you sir.'

With the middle aged men he shook hands. With the other greybeards he embraced and laughed. There were three minutes to go and still the faces were changing. Some who were outside were now inside, and those inside now outside.

'Allah tumar shateh!'

God be with you.

Suddenly the train jerked. Coolies shouted frantically, wanting to be paid, grabbing their money and making a dash for the door. Everyone was waving, shouting, up and down the train doors were slamming. With a jolt, we started to roll, we were off.

As the journey progressed things settled down. The grandmother removed her black chador like a butterfly emerging from a cocoon. She revealed herself in pastel roses on white silk. One man, who kept falling asleep, was given a bed quickly made up on the floor. The day was becoming hot, burnt dusty air rushed in through the windows. All activity had stopped as the temperature rose. We sat blankly, trying to cope with the stultifying heat. The grandmother sat cross legged on the bench opposite me, as still as a meditator. I watched her as the hours passed, she sat with a calm authority that transcended the crowded compartment. A child climbed across the bodies and curled up in her lap. I slipped in and out of sleep. I had endlessly to shift my position against the dull, hot contact of the bodies pressed against mine. At moments it felt intolerable, unbearable, I thought I would have to scream or jump up. But the moments passed and I would fall back into an exhausted sleep. Finally the evening came with a stupendous sunset. The colour broke over me like a slow wave. I was happy again, I was in the right place again. It felt like slipping on an old and familiar coat. I felt I was going home. By eleven every possible horizontal surface was occupied by sleeping bodies. Many were curled up in the filth on the floor. The train tore recklessly through the night, stirring up clouds of dust which buffeted the carriages. My eyes were dry and gritty, my hair felt like the stuffing in a very old armchair. In the half light I wrote a poem in my diary.

> "*I have no more dreams now, beyond this dream*
> *No more fears now, beyond this fear*
> *There will be no end, except this end*
> *There is no beyond, I give up*
> *I surrender.*
> *Let thy will be done*
> *on earth, as it is. . . . *"

Opposite me the grandmother sat in the darkness awake, severe. She still had not moved.

The next morning we reached Lahore and caught a bus to the Indian border. Twice before I had crossed this border going east, once with Jess and once chasing after Kate. Laurie and I found we had arrived in India on Diwali, the festival of light. It seemed a good omen. From the border a mini bus took us to Amritsar, capital of the Punjab and Holy City for the Sikh religion. We stayed for a few nights in Amritsar, at the Golden Temple Ghadwara. There was trouble in Amritsar, there had been riots the night before, shops burnt and people shot. We caught the bus to Patankhot, and at Patankhot bus station we found the McLeod bus. It was a familiar sight, the Himachal Pradesh transport company colours of blue and silver. Every day for months I had seen this bus in McLeod; it was like another old friend. A few hours later the bus drew up in Dharamsala, all but a few old Tibetan women got out. After ten minutes we were off again, zigzagging, climbing higher, the air was cool and smelt of pine forests and wood smoke. We passed the old McLeod Ganj church with its moss covered, dry stone walls and tilting gravestones, then the last incline and finally we rolled to a halt. The engine roared one final time and died into the silence of the Himalayan evening.

Laurie and I took a room at the Kokonoor hotel. The room had two beds and a view out over the plains. We set off the next morning to Bhagsunath, a riverside Indian hamlet along the valley. As we walked we fell in with a group of young Tibetan women. One was carrying her baby in a blue plastic bucket of washing. She fished him out and gave him to me to carry. We walked along in the sunshine, the baby gurgled happily on my shoulder, the Tibetan girls chattered loudly, laughing at my obvious inexperience of handling babies. Above us the snow was blowing in plumes off the high peaks and around us the rice fields were green in the sunshine. We arrived at the ancient Hindu Temple that clung to a rocky bank. A steep path from the temple led down to the river. We found a place to wash on a flat rock between house sized boulders. We spent the morning by the river, with yellow bars of Sunlight soap, pounding the dirt of the Karachi express from our clothes.

In the afternoon I went to the 'Inji Gompa' or foreigners' monastery. I was thinking maybe I could get a room there. It was a series of simple one room houses up in the woods above the village. The westerners who had taken Tibetan robes lived there along with others seriously involved in Tibetan Dharma. I walked down the path to the houses. It was very silent with only the swish of the wind through the trees. The first person I met, sitting in her door way, staring anxiously out into the abyss, smoking a cigarette held in stiff fingers, was Lucy, my old neighbour from Balcony house.

'Hello Lucy,' I said, and she looked up startled.

'Oh,' she whispered, smiling apologetically, 'Hello.'

'I've just got back,' I told her, 'I've been in Europe for the last year and a half.'

After a pause she whispered, 'I went to Bhodgaya and got teachings from His Holiness.'

Lucy did not know if there were any rooms available. She told me I needed to see Tony, an English monk, Abbot of the Inji Gompa. Instead I found Sara, an English Tibetan nun. She was also sitting on the step of her earth floored room, looking out at the clear blue sky through the pines. We began talking.

'There is a lot of suffering in the west,' I said.

'I went back,' Sara told me, 'I needed to get money together. I stayed with friends in London. They weren't suffering particularly,' she said, 'in fact the contrary was true. They had rather good lives. Rather than the Dharma, they took refuge in possessions, parties and friends. They lived in a kind of God realm. One thing flowing into the next.'

She spoke with a gentle humour.

'There's nothing wrong with all that,' she went on, 'I had a cottage in Norfolk. I lived there for a while. I did my weaving and I was quite happy there, enjoying the countryside. I could easily live like that.'

'But you have taken robes,' I said.

She looked down at her robes, almost surprised, 'Oh the robes don't matter much to me. It's just this is the way I want to spend my life, meditating, being alone. That's why I'm here.'

Her words left me disturbed. Was that why I was there? Was that why I had come back? To meditate. To be alone. Was that how I wanted to live? Did I want to live the life of a recluse? I knew I didn't; I knew I wanted to be involved with life, but the call to meditation kept me in a limbo, neither renouncing nor in the world. Moving to the Inji Gompa suddenly took on another dimension. It was like going into retreat, it was not just a place to live.

Back at the Kokonoor Hotel I found Laurie sitting on his bed writing.

'When I do go back to England, I shall definitely work with children.' I told him.

I had been planning this during the walk back.

'You're always making plans,' said Laurie, 'all the things you will do to somehow improve yourself and stop your suffering. But it just isn't like that.' The fantasy slipped and uncertainty rushed in to fill the gap.

'It's as if there are two people in you,' Laurie told me, 'one is wild, intense, full of crazy wisdom and extremely loveable, the other is pious, sensible, sentimental and rather sickly.' Then he looked at what he had been writing. 'You've got to learn to love your Dukkha,' he said, 'I'm sure of this.'

Understanding came in a rush. I had been trying to escape suffering through meditation. I was still trying to get somewhere else. But to love your Dukkha! Not to escape from it, but to welcome it, take it full on, knowing that suffering, dissatisfaction, insecurity, along with their counterparts, are the human condition, they are the truth. The truth is not beyond confusion, the truth is in it.

'Laurie,' I said, 'but what about the people who don't do all this suffering? They have jobs, or go travelling, they make decisions, they have relationships. It doesn't appear particularly complicated, their lives are not full of confusion and pain.'

'No,' said Laurie, 'it isn't like that. Mostly they are sleeping. You hurt so much because you are changing so fast.'

My journey was like a seed. I carried it and could not ignore it. I was beginning to feel the meaning in it. The usual flow of crazy thoughts, speculations, hopes and fears went on, but there was now a new line running parallel to the old. Something that saw the self, but was not quite of that self. It was as if, at last, a green shoot had burst through. I lay back on my bed and knew there was to be no going back.

Then the right day arrived. I'd been planning to go up into

the mountains and the weather, that had been grey and over-cast, suddenly cleared. I packed the food that had been wait-ing on a shelf into my rucksack, and set off to Triund and perhaps beyond. During the long walk up the valley the air became noticeably colder. Above me there was fresh snow on the peaks with the first falls of the coming winter. At Triund I stopped for lunch, made a twig fire and fried some eggs. I ate them from the pan sitting on the brink of the valley. In front of me the great rock wall, the face of the Dahuladar peak, now covered in snow, towered thousands of feet straight up. After lunch I set off for Laka, a cluster of crude stone huts, used by shepherds during the summer. Laka was at the foot of the Dahuladar peak, on the last areas of meadow before the rock face. As the path climbed higher up the ridge there was a lot of snow and my feet, in cheap ordinary shoes, were becoming cold and wet. I turned and walked back to Triund.

When I came out onto the meadow above Triund I saw, far below, that the old bungalow had been occupied by a crowd of Indian army soldiers. I decided I would stay in a cave; this would be my homage to Milarepa, the great cave dwelling Tibetan Yogi. I found a small cave just big enough for me to lie down in. It was a dirty and uncomfortable place, but it was silent and intensely still. I lit a fire but the smoke made my eyes stream, driving me out into the cold evening air. When dark-ness fell I went to bed. I slept fitfully, endlessly waking, cold and shivering. The ground was hard and as I had no ground sheet or insulation, the cold penetrated up through my worn sleeping bag making it nearly impossible to get warm.

In the morning there was ice on the puddles outside. I col-lected some snow to make tea. After breakfast I decided to see if I could get to Laka while the snow was still crisp. I packed all my stuff, put on my pack, and set off up the path into the empty snowy land. The morning sun bathed the world in delicate light touched with gold. The mountains, the forest, the rocks were so silent it hissed in my ears. The silence and the grandeur of the mountains bathed in golden early light, massive and still, made me feel like an intruder. I felt as if I were corrupting the silence with my panting, noisy mind. I reached a crest and found I was following wild cat prints across the crisp, morning snow. It was sparkling blue, hurting my eyes and dazzling me into seeing rainbows. The path left the crest and I began to descend into the empty land on the far side. The virgin snow cracked under my weight. There was no other sound. I looked ahead and I could just make out the tiny stone huts far away across the snow at the foot of the towering wall of rock. The snow was getting deeper and my shoes and socks were already wet, my feet painfully cold.

I was way past the point where Saddhus had left their iron tridents stuck in rock pile shrines beside the path, daubed in vermilion, tied with tatty pieces of red cloth. God knows where they went, leaving their three pronged iron power symbol behind. Perhaps beyond to where such symbols had no meaning. Beyond that point, beyond that point and I was so small and so utterly alone that the sense of me seemed about to atomise out into. . . . But still I carried on with a scarf tied across my eyes and the silence getting bigger. I found myself clambering over boulders hidden beneath the snow, not being able to find where to put my feet. When I missed I sank up to my thighs. I looked ahead to the tiny desolate huts and stopped, suddenly afraid. I turned and started to labour back, almost panicky, snow-blind, half crazy, running away, struggling back up and past the wild cat prints and then down towards Triund again, a safe place, a place to stuff my face with my last fried eggs and salty bread, a place this side of beyond.

I stayed four days in the cave at Triund. I lived on porridge and tea, meditating in the day and suffering at night. The moon rose each night above the mountains, and with it came a roaring cold wind that drove me into the damp, cold darkness. By the fourth day my porridge oats were finished, so I packed up and set off back down the mountain. I was dirty, smelling of wood smoke, feeling happy and absurdly free. I reached the first chai shop on the outskirts of the village, drank several hot cups of chai and devoured a packet of Glucose biscuits. Then on down to the Kokonoor where I met Laurie and exchanged poems and news. That night the moon was too bright to sleep, and Laurie and I walked through the woods in the eerie light. Monkeys screeched, dogs barked and crows called, harshly unnatural in the darkness.

The Dalai Lama was coming back from a European tour and there was great excitement in the village. The main street was decorated with prayer flags, tankas and embroidered silk. To pay our respects we joined the Tibetans, all dressed in their best traditional clothes; crowds stood on each side of the road. Between our palms we held the traditional white Kata scarf of greeting, flowers and sticks of burning incense. A cheer went up as his car drove past, and the Dalai Lama was waving and smiling through the smoked glass. Back at the Kokonoor, Laurie told me he was going into retreat for ten days. He had the use of a retreat hut up in the forest above Balcony House. I had already decided to go and sit a course with Goenka in Jaipur, but it did not start for another two weeks. I knew that Laurie and I would go our separate ways at some point, but the prospect scared me. It was as if we had been on the journey back west together. We had shared the same language in a foreign land. With Laurie I knew the true from the false. But now we were back in India I felt the loneliness and fear lurking, like bullies, waiting to get me once my friend had gone.

'I'll probably go travelling, to Mandi and Kulu, until the

course begins in Jaipur,' I said without confidence.

It was better than saying, I'm scared.

'Maybe we'll meet at Dharmagiri,' said Laurie.

'Maybe,' I replied, but it all seemed so uncertain.

We embraced, Laurie swung his tatty backpack over one shoulder and with a smile he was gone. I wandered around McLeod for a few days waiting to leave. I didn't particularly want to, but having decided that I should, I felt obliged to comply with my own plans. I walked down to the main Temple outside the village and spun the prayer wheels. Back in my room I read and reread a poem by Gerald Manley Hopkins.

> '. . black, white, right, wrong;
> reckon but, reck but, mind
> but these two; ware of a world where
> but these two tell, each
> off the other; off a rack
> where, self-wrung, self-strung, sheathe
> and shelterless, thoughts
> against thoughts in groans grind.'

In the evening, sitting alone in a restaurant, I accepted an offered chillum. It was two years since I had smoked a chillum, and the quantity of hashish knocked my world view for six. I found myself completely alone, in a world full of loud and painful thoughts, viewing the people around me across a chasm, as if looking the wrong way through a telescope. That night my dreams were full of chaos and fear, accusations and misunderstandings. There were great black spiders inside my shoes, which hopped out and scuttled away. There were drunks, ugly and crude, who mocked me. Yet the dream ended very peacefully with a sense of something having passed away, as if purged. I awoke the next morning to find the world was entombed in thick mist. There was a bus to Mandi leaving from Dharamsala at eleven. After breakfast I paid my bill at the Kokonoor and set off down the steep back road to Dharamsala. As I walked down through the mist the remnants of my motivation to leave drained out of me. When I got to the Tibetan Library complex, just above Minu cottage, instead of going on to the bus I took a room at the library guest house. Another wave was coming at me, rearing up from my unconsciousness. I could see it coming and by now I knew it well. There was little I could do but let go into it. I had nowhere to go and nothing to do. Finally, I made no plans. That night my dreams were vivid. I was walking in darkness through tightly spaced wine glasses by torch light. I stumbled and fell on them, but oddly none broke. Unseen voices warned me to be careful. The next day I walked back up the hill to McLeod and took a room at the Green Hotel. That night more intense dreams came. I was in a car driving fast along the edge of a cliff, I was in the back trying to seduce a girl and at the same time I was furious with the driver for driving so dangerously. But then suddenly I knew it was all me, and looking at the other people in the car I was overcome by compassion, and a great sense of regret and sadness.

I set off south to Jaipur by bus, arriving the day before the course. It was my birthday, and I wandered the back streets in the warm evening, drank sweet warm milk and ate sticky Indian sweets. The meditation course was intense. By now I was used to the process. I worked hard, I was not interested in getting lost in dreams. I had sat fifteen courses over the last two years. I could easily sit quietly without agitation. I was not bothered with doubts about Goenka, he had become incidental. The technique I knew was just a tool. The truth was that I was alone in a dark cell with the entirety of who and what I was. I went deeply inside, to the dark emptiness within, watching the flow of sensation, of thoughts, sensing the parameters of my existence. I had been to this place many times by now, staying with subtle sensations, penetrating the body mass with concentration, absorbed into the inner flow of life, seeing how thought arose with sensation. Yet for all that there was still always a sense of waiting for something to happen. The sense of observing myself meditating, of someone in the back ground waiting to achieve something. I felt happy while I was in the silent sanctuary of the centre, but after the course finished and I returned to Jaipur city I felt vulnerable, raw and ill-equipped to deal with the world. I found Jaipur overwhelming, a seething noisy chaos.

The meeting place for the course had been in the cloistered courtyard of an ancient Jain Daramsala in the city. I decided to see if the Jain management would let me stay. I received a luke-warm reception, but, after consultations, they told me I would be permitted to stay for a few days. I seemed to be the only person there. That evening I went to a restaurant to eat, but the food was very rich and I could eat little of what I ordered. I woke in the night and had to dash for toilets where I was violently ill with diarrhoea and vomiting. The latrines were particularly desolate, the walls and floors were concrete and the only light was from a solitary bulb. Squatting over a black concrete hole in the semi darkness at two in the morning, my body contorted by the spasms of vomiting and simultaneous diarrhoea, I felt very, very far from home.

After several days recovering I decided to go back to Mount Abu on my way to Igatpuri. I caught the overnight train south, and when I arrived, I checked into the Lake View Hotel where I had been on my previous journey. I was crashing down, great waves of loneliness came at me. I could not find any consolation in meditation, the words in my books became hollow, the room was dirty and sordid, my life, my journey seemed utterly futile. But I made no plans. That night I was wracked again by vomiting and diarrhoea. By midnight I was shivering uncontrollably and was so weak I could hardly stand. I managed to get back to my sleeping bag where I fell into a comatose sleep. The next day I was still unable to walk any distance and I drank only water. The following day I managed a trip to the bazaar to buy some papaya. My mind was still dark and I felt isolated, the people in the bazaar seemed careless and greedy, interested only in money. Everywhere there was poverty and the ever present smell of old urine. I found it all disgusting.

A day later I was well enough to go out and spend some time at one of the chai shops in the village, where I met another traveller. He had been travelling for five years, and for a while had lived by begging. His eyes were filled with a great sadness.

'I came to India with my girlfriend but she wanted to have a good time,' he shook his head as he remembered her, 'I could not give her the good times she wanted. She left me, but I am not angry, I understand.' he looked at me, 'you know what I mean when I say I have the dialogue within.'

'Yes,' I said, 'I know about the dialogue within.'

'Then you also,' he told me with a sad smile, 'ask the questions that bring unrest.'

After another fifteen hour bus journey I arrived at Igatpuri. Laurie was there, and we were put in the same cell together. Once again I went deep into myself, but once again when the course was over I felt vulnerable. I had no idea what to do or where to go. I knew Krishnamurti was speaking in Madras, and after reading his words for the last four years I wondered if, perhaps, it was time to hear him speak. After a few days I said good-bye to Laurie again and caught the train to Bombay. I went straight to the Victoria terminal booking office. It was Tuesday and Krishnamurti was starting his talks on the Thursday, which happened to be Christmas day. It was a thirty-six hour journey. If I could leave that night I had just enough time to get there. When I got to the counter my plans were dashed.

'All trains fully booked,' the clerk told me.

'But the tourist quota?' I asked.

'Tourist quota also fully booked,' said the clerk.

'But I must get to Madras,' I said despairingly.

He looked at me for a moment, 'you can make application for special circumstances quota.'

Following his directions I went to the station master's office expecting a quiet interview, but found instead a crowd of thirty or forty people pushing around the door, all frantically waving telegrams. The telegrams all looked oddly alike. I managed to read one, it said - Father died come at once - I looked at several others, they all seemed to say the same. Being India I was sure they were from rent-a-telegram. The door of the office kept opening and a middle aged man looked out, triggering a wild crescendo of pleading voices and waving telegrams. He would choose someone, seemingly at random, and they would be issued with a ticket. The next time the door opened I joined the throng. When he looked my way I cried passionately,

'Please! I must be in Madras by the twenty fifth.'

To my astonishment he beckoned to me. I had done it. I was to be one of the chosen few.

In the early hours of the second night of the journey I awoke in the half light. The train had stopped. My berth was at the end of the carriage above the aisle. I stretched my legs out. Then the door slammed, a whistle blew, a voice shouted and the train began to move. With the comforting rhythmic motion of the carriage restored, I prepared to go back to sleep. I turned on my side tucking in my legs. Below me in the dim light stood a slim, young western woman. But she was no traveller; this woman was elegant. She stood beside a large suitcase. Her clothes were stylish and she wore leather shoes with slightly high heels. She was improbably beautiful with olive skin and short dark hair. I watched her in disbelief. Sensing my gaze she looked up.

'Hello,' I said quietly, 'where have you just come from?'

''ello,' she said with a strong French accent, 'I have had a tewible time. I have just come to India from France, but I got down from ze train at ze wrong station. So I wait for ze next train. But then they will not let back onto first class, they say I have the wrong ticket. What can I do? I get zis ticket in France and so,' and she shrugged prettily, ''ere I am.'

She was flirtatious, outrageously sexy.

'But what are you doing in India? Why are you here?'

I wanted to ask. Are you real?

She looked up and smiled, 'I am studying ze erotic Indian sculpture,' she said her eyes intense and beautiful, 'I just love zees erotic sculpture so much.'

I became very aware of my sensations as I looked down on this sex bomb, this goddess who was crazy about erotica, who had been dropped at my feet in the middle of India. We talked on together, it was strangely intimate, the dim lights, the middle of the night, the surrounding sleeping people. We spoke softly, just the two of us, me on my shelf, bare footed, old canvas bag, and she all manicured and smooth.

'Have you seen zees sculptures?' she asked, 'No? Oh but you must, you should come...'

She told me how she would be getting off the train in a couple of hours, near some ancient ruined temples famed for their erotic carvings. I told her that I was going to Madras to hear Krishnamurti speak, that the talks began the next day.

'Why not come with me?' I asked hopefully, 'we could come back together after the talks and see the sculptures.'

'No,' she smiled sweetly, invitingly, 'I don't have zee time...'

I was worried about how she would survive being in India. I began to consider going to visit temples as a chaperone, to look after this vulnerable beauty. I thought I could perhaps hear Krishnamurti talk another time. But when the train stopped a few hours later, I hung on to my shelf and wished her well.

Chapter 11

The Krishnamurti talks were in the gardens of the Vasanti Vihara beneath large trees full of bird song. It was evening and the sun was setting. There was a large crowd, at least a thousand, sitting on rugs facing a dais. Krishnamurti came out, he was small and looked quite frail but he walked fast, straight to the podium. There was no sense of here I am. He looked like a man with a job to do. He was dressed in a traditional white kurta shirt and cotton trousers. Once he had settled on the podium, cross legged on a simple white mat, he looked around at the crowd as if taking us in. When he began to speak, his voice was a surprise; it was a cultured English voice, the voice of an elderly professor.

'I don't know why are you all here?' he asked. 'It is a rather important question to ask. Why each one of us is here? With what intention, and with what purpose.....?' He went on, 'We are going to talk over things together. This is not a lecture, but a meeting together, a conversation, like two friends, sitting under a lovely tree, looking at the world.... And what is the world? Who has created this world? Why has man become as he is? Thoughtless, careless, indifferent and without love? Why the endless wars, violence and division?'

'Don't listen and agree or disagree,' Krishnamurti went on, 'but look at yourself. Your own life. What you are. Find out for yourself. Do not accept something because the speaker says it, or because it is in some book, but look, examine, question. You have to doubt, to hesitate. You have,' he paused as if looking for the right word, 'you have.... to care.' He spoke the word with intensity, with such passion, that it seemed to encompass all the suffering of the world.

At that moment I knew what I had been missing from the Vipassana teachers, from the practice of meditation with a technique, it was feeling, it was passion. It was to look with the whole of one's mind and heart, and care for the beauty and suffering of the world. The path and the goal the same.

As we left the Vihara after the hour-long talk, a collection of village women had congregated at the gates to beg from the departing crowd of middle class Indians. They had brought their children who thought it was all great fun. A woman with a baby on her hip and a little girl tagging behind followed me along the pavement towards the rickshaws.

'Sir. Sir. Baksheesh, sir' she whimpered.

I gave her a few coins and got into the rickshaw, but she did not give up.

'Sir. Baksheesh.'

The rickshaw began to move and she began to jog beside it faster and faster. The baby was beaming at me, with his head wobbling about, and the little girl was running behind laughing a crazy, whoop-it-up laugh. They were having a whale of a time. I laughed with the child and then the mother, becoming conscious of the absurdity of her theatrical begging, started laughing too. For a few seconds we shared the joke as equals, then the rickshaw pulled away.

'Thought,' said Krishnamurti the next evening, 'is responsible for all the misery in the world. One idea against another, one belief against another, thoughts against thoughts. Perpetual wars between human beings. Thought, in its search for security, has divided us into religions, into nations. But it has also built the great cathedrals, temples and mosques. It has brought great benefits through hygiene, communications and rapid transport. But,' he went on, 'thought has also created havoc in our daily lives. In our relationships, between man and woman. Then, having created humanity's problems, thought has tried to solve them. It has created all the systems, the techniques, the leaders, the Gurus .... But still we remain what we are. A little more observant perhaps, a little more kindly, but basically what we have been since the beginning of time' he continued, 'If you can see that thought is the source of all mankind's misery, not intellectually, not as an idea or a conclusion, but see the fact, then you can ask a completely different question - which is; if thought is not the instrument by which we can solve our problems, then what is?'

This was a question he left hanging, and then changed his approach.

'Relationship,' he said, 'is the mirror in which we can see ourselves as we are. There is no escape from relationship, it is the basis of all life. We have to learn to observe, how we look at the world, how you look at a tree, one of the most beautiful things on this planet, or the new moon.'

He stopped, looking around, 'are you following all this?' he asked, 'are you interested in all this? You sit at the bank of the river and you look at the river, but you do not join the river, take part in that movement which has no end.' and his voice cracked, full of emotion.

'So,' he continued, as if shaking off a sense of hopelessness, 'to understand all this you have to understand what effort is. And see that where there is a cause for suffering, there must be an ending of that cause. So what is the cause of suffering?' he looked out at the sea of waiting faces, 'please don't wait for the speaker to tell you!' he begged, 'you have to find out!'

I sat and looked inward for all I was worth.

'One of the causes,' continued Krishnamurti, 'may be the desire to become. I am greedy, I will become not greedy. I am violent and I will become non-violent. And all becoming is a process of time, of thought, moving from this to that. And in that movement there is always the conflict. Conflict between what is and what should be.'

The talks were spread over two weekends. During the week between there were two morning sessions of questions and answers. The next morning, after one of these, I sat in the gardens of the Vasanti Vihara with Jacob, an Australian who had come to Krishnamurti after ten years of Transcendental Meditation. I liked him. He was in his forties, nearly twice my age. I had talked with him a lot about meditation and technique. Often when Jacob spoke I found he had a quality that seemed to challenge me. He sounded so sure and his sureness threatened me, I wanted to get the better of him, I wanted to put him down.

We were sitting on the grass in the shade of a large tree, the warm wind rustled the leaves. We were talking about leaders.

'All politicians and leaders, are a product of the people they lead. People create their own leaders,' said Jacob.

He sounded so sure, I felt angry.

'Oh sure!' I scoffed angrily at him, 'I suppose the miners, the people stuck in high rise apartments, on the dole with no work, they wanted Mrs Thatcher.'

Jacob looked at me and said amiably, 'if you talk to me like that, the only response I have is to get up and walk away.'

Whether it was Jacob, or whether it was because we were in the proximity of Krishnamurti, I do not know, but something happened to my mind in his reply to my hostility. It stopped. The was just silence and space. In that instant for the first time in my life, I saw with complete clarity the nature of thought. I saw how it divided, how it isolated, how it measured and how it was full of fear. And I realised thought could never love, that was the most shocking. Thought is never love. In the shock of the moment of insight something happened physically. With an intense flow of sensation it felt as if a door opened in the bottom of my brain and consciousness, which had been locked up in my head, a prisoner of thought, poured down into my heart.

During Krishnamurti's last talk I felt a quality in the air, an intensity that pervaded the whole meeting. Towards the end he began to talk of death, love and meditation.

'So what is meditation?' he asked, 'not how to meditate, which is the most stupid question. In meditation there is no structure, there is no measurement. There is no movement. I am this, I will become that. When the mind is thinking in terms of better, then there is no meditation. You can sit cross legged, practise techniques, yoga, all kinds of control, but if there is control, there is measurement.' He was losing the crowd, they had looked at their watches, they knew it would soon be time to go home. He looked in wild exasperation at us, and demanded, 'Are you interested in all this? Do you see the importance of this?' Then with an air of weary detachment continued, 'I don't think you do, but allow me another few minutes.'

'So,' he continued, 'in meditation there must be no effort. Meditation is not separate from daily life, it is not going off into a little corner and doing what ever it is you do, sitting quietly for twenty minutes. Meditation is when there is a mind that belongs to no group, obeys no authority, is completely free. A mind that has a quality of intelligence that has nothing whatsoever to do with cleverness. And in that intelligence there is attention. If you attend with your whole body, your nerves, your eyes, attend completely, then you may come upon a quality, an unfathomable silence, that has never been touched by thought. Only then is there that which man has searched for since time immemorial. Something sacred, something nameless, something supreme.'

The last talk had come to an end. I sat immobile, eyes closed. I didn't want to move. I didn't want to break the spell and return to the world. But the crowd, realising the show was over, leapt to its feet and began flooding, chattering loudly, to the exits. The passing people knocked against me as they went. I knew it was meaningless to hold on to the experience, the Krishnamurti darshan. I opened my eyes and the podium was empty. It was all over. I no longer had any reason to stay in Madras.

The 139 Varanasi-up Express clattered across the endless plains, over wide and beautiful rivers, through groves of trees, through fields of different colours, with palms and hay ricks, cows and peasants. Sharp hills projected out of the flat land like stones stuck in a beach. They were purple in the heat haze, dotted with white shrines. Every three or four hours the train arrived in a large town. The buildings closed in. In the station, cries of vendors filled the air. Children came through the carriage, their eyes expressionless, wearing only filthy rags- Sir, Sir, Sir, probed their young insistent voices. They got left overs, a few paisa. As I was white and sitting in an aisle seat, I was an easy target. I gave a few paisa to each child that came past. Then one small boy stopped by me. Hand held out, his manner was like all the others, a prepared, practised, monotonous, Sir Sir Sir. In the centre of his stomach a ball of his intestines protruded.

'Hospital,' he said, 'Hospital...fifty rupees...sir... Hospital....' and as he spoke he scraped at the flesh with his nail and it began to bleed.

He held out his bloody fingers in front of my face. It could have been a trick, something stuck on, but it looked real. It was more likely he had found that self mutilation was good business. I gave him five rupees and he moved on. I was shaken, half angry, half devastated. The next moment a dreadful cripple came dragging himself through the filth on the carriage floor, past the feet of the clean and comfortable passengers. It was too much and I began to cry. I got up and went and stood by the open door of the now moving train. I wanted to be alone and let the tears pass. A man came and stood near me.

'From which country are you coming?'

'What is the purpose of your visit?'

'Are you married?'

All the usual meaningless questions.

'What are you doing in your country?'

'Studying,' I replied, for want of a better explanation.

'What subject? Which class?' he demanded.

Then I saw it was my own wish to be seen as respectable. In a world full of hunger, hatred and suffering I was concerned about a false image in the minds of others.

'I'm doing nothing in my country,' I said simply, 'nothing.'

Without a word the man just turned and walked away.

It was mid January when I arrived back in Bhodgaya. The village was packed with pilgrims. It was the high season when Buddhist teachers and, in particular, the Dalai Lama, came to Bhodgaya to teach. His presence brought thousands of Tibetan and Himalayan pilgrims from places like Bhutan, Zanskar and Ladakh. They were a wild lot, wearing funky mountain clothes and smelling strongly of sheep. On my last visit the village had had a handful of resident beggars, all lepers, who had sat by the road and plied a quiet trade. Now, the village was home to hundreds of beggars, professionals who toured India's pilgrimage sites. They were sitting on every roadside and in long lines outside the stupa gates. I managed to get a room at the Burmese Vihara. My money was at the point of no return; I probably had enough to get back overland, but I had no plans to go back. I could not see any reason to return to the west.

A ten day retreat was starting at the Thai temple led by Christopher Titmus, an Englishman who had been a forest monk in Thailand for many years. I had heard his name mentioned before from friends at Dharmagiri. I joined the retreat at the Thai temple, and was given a straw mattress in the temple cellars with thirty other men. The retreat was similar in form to the Goenka courses, with silence and sitting, but the practice was different. The breath was observed not at one point, but just as the breath, the whole process of breathing, just knowing that you are breathing. The thoughts and sensations were also observed, but again with out a specific system, just watching, being aware of what was happening. He also asked us to accept all sensory perception within our field of awareness. It was bare attention to the 'what-is.' I enjoyed this approach, the openness of it, the no-technique technique.

After the retreat I found the Burmese Vihara had been booked as the venue for a Goenka course, to be led by one of his western assistant teachers. The Ghandi ashram had kindly let out their large hall as a temporary dormitory for all those made homeless by the closing of the Vihara. I became involved in helping organise the move. Once the hall was set up it looked like a refugee camp, and was the biggest dormitory I had ever slept in. There were a hundred straw mattresses in long rows on the floor. It was coming up to full moon and the energy in the village was intense. During the day the Dalai Lama was giving teachings in the grounds of the Stupa to a capacity crowd. I had gone, but the teachings were in Tibetan and I could only take so much of being jammed in with the crowds. In the heat, the smell of sheep was overpowering.

One evening I wanted to get away from the intensity of the crowded village and returned to the Thai temple. The wide grounds were empty. As I walked towards the cool steps of the temple building, the great sweeping roofs cast shadows in the moonlit silence. I sat down and watched the full moon. After I had been sitting alone for a while a woman appeared, whom I recognised from the meditation course. She was tall, with naturally brown skin and long hennaed hair. She was very beautiful and rather glamorous. She sat down beside me and began to tell me about her life. She was Brazilian and had been the wife of a millionaire, but had left him to become a Rajneesh Sanyassin. She told me of her journey. I was shy with her, like school boy. Her life of wealth and lovers seemed far removed from my own rather lonely and austere existence. She came and knelt in front of me, taking my hands and looking long and deep into my eyes.

'On the retreat,' she told me, 'I looked around the hall and I tried to decide who I would like to be with, who of all those people would lay the least trips on me.' she smiled gently, 'I picked you. Do you know why?'

'Why?' I asked.

'Because you were the most innocent.'

She looked into my eyes.

'How does that make you feel?' she asked.

'Partly afraid,' I replied, 'but mostly incredibly good.'

'People need to hear nice things about themselves,' she told me, 'it is like vitamins.'

I felt I must be overdosing.

'Do you know about your sexuality?' she asked.

'Not very much,' I replied, 'I haven't had much opportunity.'

'You should find out,' she said holding my hands, 'you should find out how much you are man, and how much you are woman.'

Then she asked, 'Do you feel attracted to me?'

I felt her warm hands and got a rush of excitement.

'Now that you've asked me, I do now.'

She looked into my eyes and said nothing, allowing the attraction to hover between us. She got up gently, letting go of my hands. She looked up at the moon, which beamed down like a heavenly spot light, gave me a smile and was gone. My own sexuality was like a darkness within me, it was all mixed up with fear and love and loneliness. The only way, I realised as I sat there, to go into that part of myself, was through relationship. That was the only way. I knew also that I was ready, my heart had been opened.

The next evening I went to the Thai temple again. I wanted to know more, to have more vitamins, but predictably, she was not there. The same evening I heard that teachings were to be given at a recently built Tibetan Monastery outside the village. These teachings were to be in English, and were said to be very powerful. I arrived late and as the room was packed, I only just squeezed in at the back. The Rimpoche was sitting at the front, he was alert and did not refer to scriptural writings. These teachings had a different quality to the other Tibetan teachings I had witnessed at the Tibetan Library in Mcleod. He talked about the nature of thought and the nature of awareness. As I listened I could see the whole thing he described, my mind had become extraordinarily clear and empty. He was describing what was happening to me. I felt awake, completely wide open, as if conscious of every nerve in my body.

'If you can understand this,' said the Rimpoche, 'then you don't need to do prostrations, mantras, visualisations or any techniques. You can drop all that; those practices are only a preparation, they are for those who cannot understand these teachings.'

After the teachings I walked back into the village and went to Shivanath's chai shop. A group of people who had come from the Tibetan teachings were sitting at a table outside. I knew a few of them so I sat down at the table. Sitting opposite me was a young woman. As I sat there we looked across the table at each other and there was no division between us. It was as if we shared the same space. No thoughts interfered, there was a wordless meeting. It was not my imagination. It was not something put together by the mind. It was not an idea, or a description. It was alive, a fact, a movement of communication. All I had to do was stay with it. So we sat there staring into each others eyes, and I felt extraordinarily happy. A man sitting next to her looked at the two of us, from one to the other, like watching tennis.

'Wow!' he said, 'there's something going on here.'

We laughed, we knew he was right. We walked together back to the Ghandi Ashram, and in the darkness we turned and held each other. The next morning we met again. Her name was Elizabeth and she was from Germany. We walked together around the outer path of the stupa. She was as surprised as I was by the effortless openness between us. There were no protected corners, no rules, no images to hide behind.

There was to be an audience for the westerners with the Dalai Lama at the Tibetan monastery. We gathered in a large hall and filed past him. He shook hands with each of us and asked us if we were well. As I shook his hand I felt such an intensity of love, a warm compassion that burst my heart open, and as I walked away I realised I was crying. I walked over to where Elizabeth stood, she was crying too. We looked at each other and laughed, it was all so crazy and intense.

When the Goenka course finished we all moved back to the Burmese Vihara. For the first few days Elizabeth and I slept in separate dormitories, but when a double room became free I asked her to share it with me. At first when we moved in together we did not sleep together. It was not a casual relationship, and I knew that when we came to it, sex was going to bring a lot more than just pleasure. Elizabeth said she was not ready and I thought I never would be.

One evening there was a Hindu festival in the village next to the Vihara with much wild drumming. That night we slept together, uneasy about being in the Vihara as it was a monastery. We found out the next morning that the festival of the night before had been a religious festival for the fertility of the women, and the empowerment of young boys. We laughed at India's magic.

Elizabeth and I were now living together. We were a couple which was very unfamiliar for me. She told me how she had arrived in Bhodgaya. She had come to India from Germany, via Sri Lanka, three months earlier. Before leaving Germany she had finished with a destructive marriage and had given up her job as a social worker. She had travelled through India to Nepal. A friend of hers from Germany was staying at Kopan, the Tibetan monastery near Kathmandu. Although Elizabeth didn't know a great deal about Buddhism, she went to visit her, as she was looking for somewhere quiet to try to work out where she was going. She had found all the westerners staying there were taking a Tibetan meditation course, and so she was left pretty much to herself. A Rimpoche was giving audiences, and after several days she decided to go to see him. There had been four people at the meeting, and the others had all kinds of long questions about their Tibetan practice. She had not been able to follow much of it, but when they had got up to leave the Rimpoche had called to Elizabeth as she reached the door. He asked her if she had been to Bhodgaya. She hadn't even heard of Bhodgaya. The Rimpoche told her that she should go there. When she left the room, although she had had various other plans they were eclipsed, she knew she was going to Bhodgaya.

'I was surprised,' she told me, 'by just how certain I was.'

As the weeks passed by, the realisation that we were going to have to move on crept up on us. Elizabeth had a month left before her return flight to Germany from Sri Lanka. Occasionally, at odd moments, when I remembered we must part it was like being sucked empty. Like a great gulf filled with unbearable sadness. I knew that if I was to be able to love without fear I had to cross that gulf. Somehow I knew I had to let her go. It felt like part of the deal, part of why we had met. This was a beginning, not an ending. With the awareness of what would come when Elizabeth was gone I began to plan a retreat. I did not want to go back to Igatpuri with its structures, rules and technique. I did not want to practice some method; I wanted just to be somewhere alone and cross over what felt like the last charred bit of the floor I had seen in my dream.

At Shivanath's chai shop Elizabeth and I met a man who had just come from Tiruvamanali in the south of India. He had been staying at the Ashram of Ramana Maharishi, a teacher who died thirty years earlier. I did not know of Ramana Maharishi, but I liked the sound of the place. There was a sacred mountain called Arunachala. It was so sacred you could only walk on it with bare feet. On the mountain were caves inhabited by hermits and yogis. He thought I might be able to stay in one. I saw myself in a loin cloth, sitting in a cave on the sacred mountain, a yogi, a holy man. In this fantasy I was incredibly peaceful, completely in control. Our last five days in Bhodgaya we spent in room retreat. Keeping silence, watching the movements of thought and feeling. We finished on the full moon, said good-bye to our friends, gave away our cooking equipment and, rising at four thirty, headed off to Varanasi.

The south was far hotter than the north, and intensely humid. Tiruvamanali was a small country town, jutting out of the plains at the foot of a rocky hill, the sacred mountain of Arunachala. As we walked out of town, following directions for the Ramana Ashram we passed a big and ancient Hindu temple. It towered upwards, ancient grey stone, bristling with carvings, like an occult antenna. The ashram compound was outside the village at the base of the hill. We entered carefully, feeling shy, unsure of the etiquette. The temple had cool marble floors, stone pillars and wide doors and windows. At one end was a large lingam on a marble base. Brahmins, bare but for their dhotis and sacred threads, padded silently from place to place. They carried water in brass pots and bowls of smoking incense, they were busy with their rituals.

'We prefer people to write to us if they wish to stay at the ashram.' said the man in the ashram office.

'We didn't know we were coming. We only decided recently when we heard about the ashram from a friend.' I said, dreading the thought of a hotel in the town.

'Come with me,' said the administrator, and led us out of the ashram compound and across the road. We entered another area of buildings. It was quiet and shaded by large trees. There were various sized bungalows, and at one end was a long concrete building.

'That is our library,' gestured our guide, 'you are welcome to use it.'

He fished from his pocket a large bunch of keys and began opening the doors to one of the larger bungalows. He pushed the doors open.

'I hope this is satisfactory. If you need anything please come and see me.'

This was the Indian house of my dreams, with wide empty rooms and smooth, cool floors. We had our own simple bathroom, and a mesh covered veranda, but, most amazing of all, we were alone. There were no neighbours, no hotel staff, just the quiet tree shaded compound and the odd passer by. Elizabeth and I sat on the bed and hugged each other. We half expected someone to come knocking at the door. 'There's been a mistake, you can't stay here.' but no one came. That evening we sat and meditated in the ashram temple and knew we had arrived somewhere extraordinary.

At our house we were a couple. It was like playing, pretending for a few days that it had no end. We began to read about Ramana Maharishi and his teachings. As a young boy he had had an experience of dying, not of the body but of the mind, and this experience made him leave home and walk to the temple at the foot of Arunachala. He went into the catacombs under the temple and began meditating. By the time he was discovered weeks later ants had started eating his flesh. He became much revered, and was cared for by the temple priests and local people. What made him particularly unusual was that he never spoke. After five years he moved from the temple up to a cave on the mountain. He continued meditating in silence for a further fifteen years. After twenty years of silence, he began to teach. At first he taught at the cave and later, when his following grew, at the ashram, at the foot of the mountain. He lived in a small, one roomed house and continued the life of an ascetic until his death. There were many photos of him around the ashram. He had a kindly face with soft eyes, short white hair and a short beard. He had said that the experience he had at sixteen had not changed in the twenty years of silence. He had just been going into it, exploring, finding out. Ramana told his students to look and find out, 'Who am I? Who speaks? Who sees? Who thinks?' These were not questions to be answered with words. The answer was in being, not in knowelge.

We passed the days between our room, the library, the ashram and the village. Because the heat was so intense, it did not take much to fill the day. Between ten in the morning and five in the afternoon, it was pretty hard to do anything at all but read or, after lunch, doze under the fan. When we went out we spent our time sitting either in the hall with the Brahmans and their lingam, or in Ramana's small and austere one roomed house, which had been left untouched, as a shrine. Each evening we walked into Tiruvamanali to eat at one of the town's restaurants. The men who ran these places, like the priests in the temple, only wore dhotis and sacred threads. The restaurants were very different from the crummy and dirty places I had become used to. They were austere and clean, and the excellent food was served on large stainless steel plates. It was simple and vegetarian. It was more than just a livelihood for the owners, it was their way of life, their Dharma. Here in the south I saw another side to India. A Hindu tradition that stretched back, unbroken, for five thousand years.

I continued with my plan to do a long retreat lasting several months. I found a room to rent quite close to the ashram. It was at the foot of the hill, and was very simple, with only a small table and a rope charpoy bed. It was owned by a rather dubious Swami,

'I am also having other western people doing meditation in my room,' he told me.

'Did they stay long?' I asked.

'The last one was a lady from Italy,' he said quite cheerfully, 'unfortunately she went mad and was cutting herself here.' And he drew his fingers across his wrists.

A few days later I awoke before dawn. It was still dark outside. Elizabeth and I had talked several times of walking up or around Arunachala, many devotees did, like walking around the stupa at Bhodgaya, but each day we had put it off because of the heat. When I awoke this particular morning I decided that it was the right moment to walk up the hill. Slipping from the bed, careful not to wake Elizabeth, I dressed and made my way through the dark ashram to the foot of the hill. I left my sandals at the simple wooden gate and set off walking fast up the steeply winding path. I walked in long jumping strides between the large stones that had been set as rough steps. In the half light I kept my eyes focused on the stones ahead; I didn't want to step on a scorpion. The path wound several hundred feet up between rocky outcrops. It levelled out and quite suddenly I found myself on the edge of a small ridge. The hillside fell steeply away in front of me. Far below, wreathed in a haze of early mist, lay the ancient Hindu temple, monolithic and powerful. Across the plains the sun's first rays were filling the horizon with pale golds. I stood in wonderment, catching my breath from the climb. Then for a split second I saw something coming at me. It came across the plains, like an invisible wind, and hit me, tearing through my mind, stripping it of everything. I staggered back. Then it was gone and so was I. My memories, my beliefs, all the images of who and what I was had been stripped away like leaves from a tree. The created self was gone, blown away. I sat down. I had no memory nor knowledge. My consciousness was that of a child. My only thought was, 'Who will take care of me..?'

I saw a little further along the mountainside some buildings and trees nestled into the hill side. I got up and made my way along the path towards them. There was a courtyard surrounded by trees where a section of the rock face had been walled in. I entered a door in the wall and found a simple half cave, half room. In a corner there was an alcove in the rock face, it was lit by lamps and leaning against the stone was a photo of Ramana. I sat in front of it and bowed my head down to the floor. As I did so a wave of love soaked into me, seemingly pouring out from the empty alcove. I broke down and wept, sobbing incomprehensible tears, and as I wept my mind filled again with a past and future. I became again an actor in the the story of my life. Quietly I got to my feet and turned to leave. As I reached the door I heard a voice speak quite clearly inside my head. It took me completely by surprise. I had never before had a voice speak loudly inside my head. I had many of my own voices chattering away, describing, judging, planning, fantasising, but this was a clear, loud, uninvited voice and completely unexpected.

The voice simply said, 'Go back to Igatpuri.'

And as it was not what I had planned I put it aside.

There were only a few days left for Elizabeth and me. We made no plans for the future. Elizabeth knew she had to go back, I knew I had to stay. Occasionally I wondered about the instruction I had had on the mountain, 'Go back to Igatpuri'. I couldn't believe it. I couldn't see any reason to go back. I had very good reasons not to go back. I had a new understanding of meditation and I was very attached to it. So I put the guidance to one side and resolved I would stay on and do my retreat on the mountain as planned.

Finally the day came for Elizabeth's departure. We walked to the bus stand together and I saw her off on the bus to Madras. After she had gone I wandered around in a state of crazed agitation for the rest of the day. I couldn't eat, I couldn't sit still. My whole body seemed to be hurting. I stayed one more night in the bungalow with Elizabeth's absence shouting at me from every room. The next morning I moved to my yogi room along the hillside. I was now free of all worldly complications; I was a yogi, meditating on my folded blanket on the mud floor. I dipped a psychological toe into the swimming pool of feelings that boiled just beneath my conscious mind, and recoiled. I had to dive into the swimming pool. The trouble was, having set myself up at the edge, I wasn't sure I knew how to swim in such deep waters. And drowning meant a breakdown or worse, madness like the Italian girl before me with her suffering, longing for peace and bleeding wrists. After ten minutes I leapt from the cushion and rushed to the nearest chai shop.

That night I couldn't sleep. The mosquitoes came and went as they pleased, the room was suffocating and the bed was six inches too short. The next day was no better. The intensity of my feelings continued to scare me, and I began to have grave doubts about my retreat. I interpreted these as avoidance, fear to cross over, to let go of. I told myself I needed to stay, to go through the confusion, the suffering, that if I turned away from it now I'd never be free.

The instruction, 'Go back to Igatpuri,' kept coming back to me, and I began to wonder if I needed the safety and structure of Dharmagiri to go through this storm; perhaps it was just too strong to face alone, unprotected. But this idea arose at the same time as the intense fear and I could not separate the two. I found a copy of the I Ching in the library and asked for advice. I got the hexagram Modesty, but the great lone Yogi did not understand.

For the next few days I swung backwards and forwards between staying and going. When I felt okay, which was usually sitting in a chai shop, I decided to stay. When the chaos came sweeping over me, usually when I was meditating, swamping me in the most awful sensations and thoughts, I wanted to go Finally after four days, I just couldn't handle it another minute. I packed my bag and almost ran to the bus station. In Madras I went straight to the railway station and booked my ticket to Bombay. The Bombay train left the same evening at eleven. I checked into the Chandra Hotel where I had stayed during the Krishnamurti talks. I lay on my bed and the doubts returned, filling my head. Was I running away from the one place I could go through with this process? Wasn't I just reacting to fear, reacting to unpleasant sensations? I could hardly believe that having cultivated my plan for the retreat to end all retreats on the holy mountain of Arunachala, I had only managed to stay a paltry four days. Going to Igatpuri and staying at Arunachala kept swapping places in my head, both sounded completely convincing as they arose. I began to wish for a sign. Even though the first sign had been pretty unambiguous, I needed another sign. The refuge of the confused and indecisive. I imagined an old man grabbing my arm in the bazaar.

With eyes blazing, he would say, 'Go to Igatpuri!' Or, of course, he also might say, 'Don't go to Igatpuri!'

Finally, exhausted, I fell asleep.

When I awoke it was evening and the sun was beginning to set. I got up and went onto the flat roof of the hotel and stood at the balustrade looking out over the city roofs fading into the violet twilight. There was a small mosque below and the faithful were arriving for evening prayers. I had been standing there for a few minutes when a young woman came and leant on the wall nearby.

'I wonder what religion means in their lives?' she asked abstractly, not looking at me, but then she turned.

'Oh,' she said, surprised, 'I thought you were someone else.'

Since leaving Bhodgaya I had been exclusively with Elizabeth, and since her departure I had not talked or even met any other travellers.

'Are you interested in religion?' I asked her.

'Well, religion, I don't know,' she replied, 'but I have done some meditation.'

'What sort of meditation?' I asked, after a pause, interested.

'I guess you would call it Buddhist meditation,' she said carefully.

'Where was that,' I asked.

'A place called Igatpuri,' she replied, 'with a teacher called Goenka.'

That night as the train rumbled north towards Bombay I had a dream, a nightmare. I was in a house with Elizabeth, but there was something surrounding the house. Whatever it was, it was truly horrific. I could see dead and mutilated bodies that had been killed by The Thing. We tried to leave the house but The Thing, which was like some ghastly plant, had tentacles that spun out and caught hold of me. We decided to get out, to another house before it became too powerful. Having escaped and found a new house I felt safe, until I realised with sinking horror that The Thing was in the water, weaving through the pipes of the house, in fact it was everywhere, there was no escape..... I awoke with my heart pounding.

I arrived at Igatpuri and went straight to the mediation centre. It was quiet, and as an old student it was no problem to stay. I wrote a letter to Elizabeth, which I hoped would catch her in Sri Lanka, telling her where I was. Then I put away my books, went into Noble silence and began my retreat. As soon as I closed the cell door and sat on the cushion my mind went mad. This was The Thing of my dream. It went something like this. I couldn't believe I had let Elizabeth go. I had lost her forever. It was unbearable. And with the fear of losing her The Thing attacked. Anger and jealousy. I played out scene after scene where I raged, berated her, abused her, in turns wildly angry writhing with frustration, and then torn with grief at losing her. Then, when I remembered it was not reality, it was only in my head, I came back to the present. I would manage a few moments of consciousness, just feeling the pain, seeing it all, the truth in the false, the false in the truth, then I would slip off again, swamped under the storm.

At the end of the five days I was stunned, shell shocked, I wanted to leave but knew I couldn't. There was a ten day course, led by an assistant teacher starting the next day, so I signed up. Back in my meditation cell I sat through another eight days of total torment, then I cracked. I decided I had to get back to Elizabeth as fast as I possibly could, even though on one level I knew that to go back motivated by fear spelt disaster. But on day eight of the course I left for Bombay. After eight days of complete silence, confined to a dark cell, peeling the skin off my mind I went straight on to an urban train heading into Bombay. I ended up in a ghastly hotel, in a room with sweating brown walls. I sat on my bed leaning back against the wall and reeled. I had to get back to Elizabeth, I had to get back, fast. My bare back stuck to the shiny paint. I telexed my parents and asked them to send me a ticket, apologising for needing their help again. I asked them to send a Syrian Arab airways ticket as I knew it was one of the cheapest, and I gave Dharmagiri as my return address. I wrote to Elizabeth in Germany and said I was coming back, very soon. I returned to Dharmagiri. I hoped there would be a letter from Elizabeth but there wasn't. I went straight back into another retreat and another ten days of outpourings. One afternoon, as I was in the midst of a particularly anger filled internal monologue, the bubble burst. All this hatred, anger, fear and jealousy, how could I call this love? Then I no longer knew what was real and what was in my mind. I thought Elizabeth and I loved each other but now I wondered if the whole thing been a fabrication? A spiritual ego trip? Just another more subtle fantasy?

After the course finished I found a letter from Elizabeth posted from Sri Lanka.

'Dear beloved Ken ,' she wrote, 'Dharmananda.....'

This was the name I had been given as a monk in Burma. Now I cringed when I read it, aghast at my vanity.

She told me she had been very ill on arriving in Sri Lanka, but was now well enough to travel and was soon flying home. She ended the letter saying 'I am with you wherever you are.' Then she wished me Moksha, the Sanskrit word meaning enlightenment, freedom. All in all it offered not one tiny shred of reassurance. I began to wait for another letter, a reply to the one saying I was coming back, very soon. I wanted a letter saying, 'I can't wait to see you again, I want to be with you, I miss you, I need you.'

I served a course to get a break, and during this course my ticket arrived. From Bombay it was now only twelve hours to Europe. Excitedly I packed my bag and caught the train back to Bombay again. The next morning I went to the Syrian Arab airline office. As I came close to the office there was a long queue out of the door and down the street, something I had never seen before at an airline office. After a long wait I finally reached the counter and presented my ticket.

'I want to make a reservation on the next flight to London,' I said.

'All flights fully booked now until the end of June,' said the desk clerk.

June! I had been thinking about having to wait days, if not hours. But June was six weeks away, which for me might as well have been six years.

'I am sorry,' said the rather harassed clerk, 'but this is the very busy time and we only have one flight a week.'

I looked at him blankly.

'Do you wish to make a reservation?' he asked.

'God, I don't know,' I said, as my plans crumbled.

I went back out onto the street. There was to be no escape. I caught the train back to Igatpuri. At Dharmagiri there was still no letter from Elizabeth. I was worn out, exhausted by it all. I joined yet another ten day course, and finally this time it was all over. I could watch, see the whole movement of jealousy, of fear and just let it go. The process was over, The Thing had died, Elizabeth had not written and I packed my bag.

I caught the train back to Bombay again, and booked myself on to a flight six weeks ahead. I had very little money left. I knew I would have to stay at the meditation centre, giving service, but it was not what I would choose to do for six weeks. I was worn out, I had had enough silence and meditation. The train back up the ghats to Igatpuri stopped at a small station. I got out, happy to stretch my legs from the cramped third class carriage. I wandered over to a drinking fountain. As I drank the cool water I heard a voice call my name.

'Hey, Ken ! What are you doing here?'

Leaning from the door of the first class air-conditioned carriage was German Klaus, who I had last seen in France. I walked over and we exchanged greetings.

'I'm on my way back to Dharmagiri,' I told him, 'you too?'

'No I'm going to Delhi. I was at Igatpuri a few months back,' he told me, 'I've just come from Goa. Having a holiday! Now I must go back to Germany.'

A whistle blew in the distance.

'Come in and travel with me,' said Klaus, gesturing to the cool empty interior.

'But I don't have a first class ticket,' I said.

'No problem,' said Klaus, 'if there is, I pay. No problem.'

The first class air conditioned carriage was cool and quiet. There were only two others in Klaus's compartment, both business men, who eyed my threadbare cotton Indian clothes with disdain. Klaus made his living buying Mercedes panel vans in Germany and driving them overland to sell in Nepal. With the proceeds he had enough money to spend some time sitting at Dharmagiri, travel around India, fly home and buy another truck. We sat and talked for the next half hour, reminiscing about people we both knew, and the changes we'd been through since we both began meditating with Goenka. Klaus told me about how he had driven Laurie to Switzerland after the course in the south of France.

'Laurie was pretty crazy after that course,' Klaus told me laughing.

I told him about my flight, and how I would stay at Dharmagiri because I was broke. When the train stopped at

Igatpuri I got up to go.

'Look, wait a moment,' he said.

He took out his wallet and pulled out several notes.

'Take this,' he said, 'I have plenty.'

I looked at the money he held out. It was a hundred American dollars.

'Klaus!' I began, 'that's too much. No! I mean that's wonderful, I could pay you back....'

'Forget it!' he said, smiling, enjoying my confusion' just say hello to Laurie for me.'

I stayed one more night at Dharmagiri then caught the train north to Delhi. With my hundred dollars I felt rich and free. I was heading for the mountains, I was going home. I sat undisturbed hour after hour, as I had so often over the last years, staring out of the window, as the barren Indian landscape unscrolled.

I wondered about Elizabeth. I wondered why she had not written. I remembered the way we had met, just a few feet from where the Buddha became enlightened. It all seemed significant, pre-destined. There had been so many inexplicable meetings. Laurie turning up out of the blue, the Goenka student appearing when I asked for a sign in Madras. Not to mention the psychic wind on Arunachala. Now, looking back, I felt as if I had been watched over on my crazy journey, as if angels had taken care of me, helping make the connections. Something like that. I had traversed the beams in the burnt out building of my dream. I had swum across the waters of the mind to reach the heart. That had been the journey, and that journey was now over. Where there had been constant noise, now there was something else; there was the silence behind the noise.

I arrived back in McLeod Ganj in late May. Laurie had a room at Balcony house. Although I had my flight booked I didn't want to go back to the west, except to be with Elizabeth.

There was nothing else for me to go back for, so I wrote her another letter. I asked her to write and tell me how she felt, I said I needed to know before I flew back. I began to await a reply. The days passed by and the flight date came closer and closer. Each day I checked poste restante, each day without success. Finally the day came when I had to leave McLeod to travel back to Bombay if I was going to catch my flight. I sat with Laurie in the Rising Horizon restaurant, hesitating to board the bus.

'I'm going to check the post one last time,' I told him. And there the letter was.

It said everything I hoped for, and more.

'She wants to see me,' I told Laurie.

'Of course she wants to see you,' said Laurie.

We walked together to the square at the end of the bazaar. The blue and silver Himachal Pradesh transport company bus was waiting. I hugged Laurie good-bye and climbed aboard. The driver casually pulled himself into his seat and the engine roared into life. The bus swung out in a wide curve and then, like the start of a roller coaster, set off down the steep mountain road.

THE END